An English Teacher's Guide to Performance Tasks & Rubrics: High School

Amy Benjamin

EYE ON EDUCATION
6 DEPOT WAY WEST, SUITE 106
LARCHMONT, NY 10538
(914) 833–0551
(914) 833–0761 fax
www.eyeoneducation.com

For information about permission to reproduce selections from this book, write: Eye On Education, Permissions Dept., Suite 106, 6 Depot Way West, Larchmont, NY 10538.

Library of Congress Cataloging-in-Publication Data

Benjamin, Amy, 1951–
    English teacher's guide to performance tasks and rubrics, high school / by Amy Benjamin
        p.   c.m.
    Includes bibliographical references.
    ISBN 1-883001-93-5
    1. Language arts (Secondary)—Evaluation.   I. Title.

LB1631.B383 2000
428'.0076—dc21

                                                                            00-23506

10 9 8 7 6 5 4 3 2

Editorial and production services provided by
Richard H. Adin Freelance Editorial Services
52 Oakwood Blvd., Poughkeepsie, NY 12603-4112
(914-471-3566)

Dedication

In memory of my parents, Nathan and Ruth Trailezer

FOREWORD

Whether you are seasoned professional or are commencing your career, Amy Benjamin is a great coach. English and reading teachers in middle and high schools can benefit from her detailed examination of standards, rubrics, and assessment. *The English Teacher's Guide to Performance Tasks* has a wealth of concrete materials that translate immediately to daily classroom practice. With the increasing emphasis on comprehensive testing with reading, writing, speaking, and listening components in each state and in each school, educators need translations. We need to know how to understand and to integrate the demands of standards into our classrooms. Benjamin's book provides real answers to this dilemma. She provides specific performance tasks for genres ranging from journalism to classical Shakespeare. The book is an English teacher's curriculum sidekick.

Ultimately, the goal is to improve our students' performance. Clearly, Johnny cannot improve his performance if he cannot improve his ability to apply grammar and syntax to his own work. This book hands the teacher practical and workable classroom activities to assist the learners in this daunting task. In particular, the exploration and unpacking of rubrics in *The English Teacher's Guide* is enlightening. Amy encourages teachers to involve active student deployment of rubrics as a way to operationalize standards. How fortunate for our field of work that Amy Benjamin has elected to make another contribution. Her first book, *Writing Across the Curriculum*, also published by Eye on Education, has proven to be extremely helpful on the subject for secondary teachers of all subjects. For any educator wishing to extend and deepen their diagnostic, prescriptive, and instructional techniques, *The English Teacher's Guide to Performance Tasks and Rubrics* is not only a must-read, it is a must-do.

Heidi Hayes Jacobs

ABOUT THE AUTHOR

Amy Benjamin teaches English and is department leader at Hendrick Hudson High School in Montrose, New York. She holds a Masters in Educational Administration from the State University College of New York at New Paltz, and is an adjunct professor at Brooklyn College, where she teaches off campus graduate courses through various teacher centers, including Putnam/Northern Westchester BOCES. Amy runs workshops and presents at various local and national conferences. She has written several articles and books on educational topics, including *Writing in the Content Areas* (Larchmont, NY: Eye on Education, 1999).

She is recognized by the New York State Council of English Teachers as a Teacher of Excellence and by Tufts University as an inspirational teacher. She has served as a model teacher for the New York State Education Department.

ACKNOWLEDGMENTS

I wish to thank my publisher, Robert N. Sickles, for his continued support in the preparation of this book series. I am also grateful once again to Dr. Heidi Hayes Jacobs for her support and training. I appreciate the research assistance of my colleague and friend, Stacy O'Donnell. Much of my recent professional work has been influenced by Dr. Ed Vavra and Dr. Martha Kolln of the Assembly for the Teaching of English Grammar, an affiliate of the National Council of Teachers of English. Finally, I am grateful to the reviewers of these books when they were in manuscript form. Their careful attention to detail and their professional comments were most helpful.

TABLE OF CONTENTS

User's Guide

This book is intended for novice and veteran teachers of English, reading, and English as a second language (ESL). It explains how a wide variety of performance tasks and rubrics can be presented in any classroom.

Chapters 1 through 5 provide the basic terminology and theory. Chapter 1 explains what performance tasks are all about and how they differ from and dovetail with traditional forms of assessment. Chapter 2 tells you what rubrics are and the different ways of constructing them so that students and teachers have a clear understanding of what qualities of a product are to be assessed without overdirecting the student. Chapter 3 explains learning standards and their relationship to instruction and assessment. Chapter 4 discusses portfolios, a natural outgrowth of performance-based curricula, and gives examples of several types. And Chapter 5 gives a very brief overview of multiple intelligence theory.

The lion's share of this book gives you step-by-step procedures of specific performance tasks that you can apply to your classroom regardless of what text you use, what ability level of students you teach, whether you have heterogeneous groups, special education students or gifted students.

Most of the tasks are presented in this format:

1. Product: *What is the genre of the task?*

2. Directions to the students: *What is a clear and concise way to tell the students what they are expected to do?*

3. Instruction: *What do students need to know and be able to do to complete this task?*

4. Standards: *How does this task address the learning standards?*

5. Challenge level: *What is particularly thorny about this task? Who might have difficulty with it?*

6. Multiple Intelligence: *Aside from verbal/linguistic skills, what other kinds of intelligence go into this task?*

7. Scoring Guide: *What is being evaluated?*

8. Follow-up: *What related and more sophisticated tasks can follow this one?*

9. Samples of student work: *What does excellence look like? What does the work of a student with emergent skills look like? What does the work of a struggling student look like? Where are the pitfalls?*

10. Remediation: *How do I scaffold or re-present this task for students who are having difficulty with it?*

The ideas in this book will energize you and your students. They will broaden your teaching repertoire to include much more than traditional essays and tests, and they will engage your students in higher level thinking about what they read, hear, write, and say.

PART I

USING PERFORMANCE TASKS

1

THE NATURE OF PERFORMANCE TASKS

CHAPTER OVERVIEW

This chapter is a primer for English teachers who need basic information about performance tasks. This chapter answers these questions:

- How do performance tasks *differ from traditional tests*?
- What is the *role of performance task assessment* in English class?
- What are the *design elements* of a performance task?
- How does performance task assessment influence *instruction*?
- What do you need to know about *portfolio assessment*?
- What are the *time management issues* involved in using performance tasks?
- What makes a performance task *authentic learning*?
- How can you develop a *collegial review process*?

When we instruct for a performance task, we make the student an active learner and problem-solver. The task should be an integral part of a series of lessons, which comprise a wide array of methodology: direct instruction, independent reading, interaction, constructed response.

HOW DO PERFORMANCE TASKS DIFFER FROM TRADITIONAL TESTS?

A performance task is a *product that demonstrates the application of knowledge.* Allan A. Glatthorn (1999) defines a performance task as "a complex open-ended problem posed to the student to solve as a means of demonstrating mastery"(p. 18). In an English class, the product can take many forms: a writing piece, an oral report, a structured discussion, a skit, an exhibit.

Consider the traditional forms of assessment in the English class of a generation ago: the five-paragraph essay, the research paper, the short-answer test on a piece of literature, the vocabulary matching column or fill-in. Short-answer tests require finite responses within a prescribed field. They ask for bits of factual knowledge out of context. They are exactly what we mean by *inauthentic learning;* that is to say, learning that serves no purpose larger than the test itself and which is, therefore, dismissible when the test is over.

Suppose your students are reading *A Tale of Two Cities*. That's a big supposition. A more likely scenario is that you've assigned a certain number of pages to be read by certain specified dates and you want to determine whether they've done your bidding. So you punctuate the reading experience with various interim quizzes, culminating in a major unit test. These assessments are usually true/false statements, multiple choice, some fill-ins, maybe a matching column. They focus almost entirely on plot events: who did what to whom, where, and when?

As teachers, we know the shallowness, but also the usefulness, of tests of this kind. To be realistic, let's admit that the genre of the traditional short-answer literature test is not about to die unmourned and be buried in unconsecrated ground any time soon. Let's consider some of the reasons why it has survived as a staple of the secondary English class.

- ◆ Motivation

  Knowing that there's a quiz on Thursday on Chapters 1 through 7 of Book The Second, actually does motivate some students to get the stuff read. The traditional short-answer literature test has served us well and true for many generations. It has offered us a vehicle for reviewing the plot line, characters, and settings of complicated stories. It has duly punished the slothful and rewarded the righteous. It has even separated those who read the actual book from those who read the study guide. It has encouraged students to take notes on the details as they read. In short, it has told us who's been naughty and nice as far as doing the reading is concerned.

- ◆ Convenience

  Paperwork is a tyrannical master. Few of us could keep up with the amount of student writing that we *wish* we could assign. So it's unrealistic to expect us to abandon the short-answer literature test, despite its shortcomings. The traditional test gives us quick feedback: *Did the students read and understand, on (at least) a literal level?* Without this level of assessment, we can't proceed to higher level thinking anyway.

♦ Traditional Expectations

There's a good reason why the short-answer response test is called *traditional testing*. It is what many parents, administrators, and students expect, and its absence would be disconcerting. Many high stakes standardized and national tests, such as the SAT/ACT and parts of Advanced Placement exams contain multiple choice questions, and, as long as they do, we need to prepare students for them. We know that it is important to familiarize students with particular testing formats, and thus we are wise to include them in our assessment repertoire.

♦ Individual Accountability

The traditional test tells us what the student knows without assistance, copying from one's neighbor's paper notwithstanding. Inasmuch as a performance task is accomplished over time and without controlled testing conditions, we can never be certain how much help the students have received when they've completed a performance task. But a performance task, unlike a traditional test, is a learning experience *in itself*. An essential part of this learning experience *is* receiving assistance from outside sources and through communication and interaction.

Short-answer tests can also serve to scaffold learning on a higher level. The test itself, once graded, can be used as a knowledge base for a more authentic performance task later on. And, of course, the short-answer test often yields important information about reading deficiencies in students who consistently perform badly even though they think they've done the reading.

So, we are not calling for the abandonment of reading checks or unit tests. But we wouldn't want to base our curriculum on these types of assessments alone. Too often, short-answer tests on a work of literature reduce the reading experience to a shallow exercise. They don't get to the deeper experience of what literature is all about: the establishment of a relationship between the reader and the text.

Recently, I asked my tenth grade students to read *Night*, the powerful memoir by Holocaust-survivor Elie Weisel. As I was passing one of my students, Joanna, in the hall on the morning of the test, I heard her telling her resource room teacher that she had been unable to put the book down, and that it had affected her deeply. Foolishly, I administered a commercially prepared test to Joanna's class, and she failed it. She was, understandably, greatly frustrated, because not only had she read the book, but it meant a great deal to her, and was, in fact, the first book assigned to her in school that she actually read from cover to cover because she wanted to. But Joanna didn't remember many of the specific names of places or minor characters and these were on the test. She didn't remember some of the religious terminology, which was on the test. She failed to guess right in the matching column, and she found some of the multiple-choice questions ambiguous. Joanna failed the test on *Night*, and I failed Joanna by giving her a test that did not determine what I had wanted to know: *did she read and understand the book?*

Had I assessed Joanna on a reader response journal, I would have discovered that she did read and understand. But we don't always have time for lengthy constructed responses such as this. I don't think my mistake was in giving a short-answer test to learn whether Joanna had done her reading, but I do think I was wrong in taking the easy way out with this particular commercially prepared test on which many of the questions asked for trivia.

I believe that we can construct short-answer tests that serve a more meaningful purpose beyond the mere recall of detail. No one wants to see students memorizing by rote a list of characters and events as if they were learning the 50 states and their capitals. And that is not to say that memorizing facts isn't important. You do need to know the 50 state capitals for future reference. But you don't need to know the names of the 50 characters in *A Tale of Two Cities.* The following are some types of short-answer literature tests that you might want to try:

♦ Identify quotations

To read literature is to be a fly on the wall. We live and breathe with a cast of characters, and we come to know them very well, if we are attentive readers. We know that only *one* character in *Gone with the Wind* says "I don't know nothin' 'bout birthin' babies, Miss Scarlett." That's an obvious example, but when students can identify the context of a key quotation, when they can say who said it, to whom, and what the response was, then they've told us that they've understood the subtlety and relationships among the characters. They've heard the voices, and can distinguish one from another. To make this type of test a learning experience, as well as a testing experience, we can ask students to submit key quotations, that only one character could have said. When we ask them to do this in cooperative learning groups, we hear interesting and high level conversations about the nature of the characters in relation to the storyline.

◆ Put events in order

Most stories go back and forth in time, and the reader needs to follow the sequence. Asking a reader to put events in order is not asking for trivial information. This type of test is convenient to grade. It can be presented in the multiple choice format: *Which of the following events came first or last?*

◆ What happened where?

If we have visualized a story, then we know that the murder took place in the billiard room and not in the kitchen. Asking students for this information is an appropriate way to see if they've read and understood because it trains them to read *cinemagraphically*, running the movie of the mind as they read.

One more suggestion regarding traditional testing in reading: Consider allowing students to bring study cards to the test. The handwritten study cards serve a heuristic purpose because the act of making the card is the act of reviewing the literature. As long as the cards are handwritten, we know that the student has taken the time and trouble to attend to certain aspects of the reading task. Index cards are then easy to collect and review with the student, if necessary.

Students take other types of short-answer tests in English class: the vocabulary test, the spelling test, the grammar/usage test. Students are famous for getting high grades on these regurgitative tests, and then failing to use the vocabulary that they've *learned*, misspelling on Monday the very words that they spelled correctly on the quiz on Friday, and making the same grammatical mistakes that they *got right* on the grammar test on which they had to edit sentences.

Vocabulary, spelling, and usage are knowledge and skills that are useful only to the extent that we apply them to real language situations. Worst of all are lists of isolated, decontextualized *vocabulary words* or *spelling words* that are together for no particular reason. If we really feel the need to give vocabulary and spelling tests, the least we should do is give students words that bear some relationship to one another. And, we can offer opportunities for the newly learned words to be used in an upcoming writing or speaking piece.

In the English language, spelling does fall into patterns. Words aren't spelled at random, and the rules are far less capricious than an uninformed speller might suppose. If we are going to give spelling lists, we should organize them around patterns and principles: words with similar suffixes, prefixes, roots, etymology. A knowledge of phonics, as well as a basic understanding of the history and development of the English language, is far more useful than a list of 20 words a week to copy 5 times each and reproduce for the Friday quiz.

Particularly vexing to me is the spelling test that presents the student with a list of five words and then telling the student to identify the one word that is spelled incorrectly. First, we never use that format in real life. In real life, we spell a word by producing it out of our heads, not by picking it out of a list. Second, the very fact that the word is presented in printed form signals to the brain that it *is* correctly spelled. That is why, the more we look at the five words grouped together, the more they *all* tend to look right or begin to look a little funny. So, I do not recommend this highly confusing and thoroughly inauthentic method of assessing for spelling. I do recommend, if anything, asking students to spell words from dictation. Best of all, we should assess spelling the way it is actually used: by asking students to write a sentence or a paragraph that uses a given list of words that are related to one another in meaning.

As for grammar and usage, knowledge of grammatical terms is essential for an intelligent conversation about language. But we can't be satisfied that the students have *learned grammar* just because they can fix sentences, or pick out the right choices, on a worksheet. Our assessment of grammatical knowledge has to come from asking the student to write complicated, interesting, varied, and correct sentences in the context of real language. This book includes a section on performance tasks based on syntax that integrate grammatical knowledge with real writing tasks.

Traditional tests in the English class, whether they be on literature recall, vocabulary, spelling, or grammar, can certainly serve as a starting point for learning. In a dynamic English class, we must go beyond traditional tests and into assessments that reflect deeper levels of understanding.

What Is the Role of Performance Task Assessment in English Class?

Authentic tasks that are accomplished over a period of days or weeks are richer and more rewarding than traditional tests and in-class essays. Performance tasks that evoke higher level thinking allow literature and the study of the language arts to achieve their intended purpose: to connect, to communicate, to illuminate the outside world and the self.

Charlotte Danielson and Elizabeth Marquez (1998) divide performance tasks into two types: product and behavior. A *product* can be *written* or *physical*. A *behavior* can be *structured* or *spontaneous*.

In an English class, we're used to asking for a written product in various genres: a traditional five-paragraph essay, a traditional research paper (aka *term paper*), an extended paragraph, a piece of creative writing. In addition to these, we can expand the repertoire of written products to include such non-fiction genres as the user's guide, a multileveled list with various textual features, a set of directions, advertising copy, informational text with visuals, a labeled diagram. A physical product in an English class can include a props box, a miniature theatrical set, a collage or montage, a piece of art, a display. Usually, the physical product submitted for English class also contains a written component that explains it.

Danielson and Marquez (1998) point out that products that are produced outside of class and beyond controlled testing conditions are ill suited to high-stakes assessment, because we can't know the extent to which the student received assistance from other people. "For instructional purposes, most of us encourage our students to obtain as much help as they can get; students are bound to learn more from an assignment with the insights of additional people. However, for purposes of assessment we need to know what each student can do; this requirement limits the usefulness of out-of-class assignments for evaluation. When used, they should be supplemented by other sources of information (for example, an assignment given under testing conditions) of which we can be sure of authorship."

It is always difficult to tease out the student's own knowledge from that of those who helped her. This fine point is especially difficult in English Language Arts where, to a large extent, communication is not the means to an end but the end itself. This is another reason why we need to rely on a variety of assessment techniques.

Behavior is a demonstration of knowledge and understanding; we can evaluate behavior. *Structured* behavior consists of scripted activities such as performance pieces (skits, oral presentations, debates and panel discussions, recitations, interviews). *Spontaneous* behavior consists of peer interactions in literature circles or ad hoc discussion groups, questions and responses to the teacher, attentiveness and note-taking behavior, use of free-reading time and library time. Many teachers give grades based on class participation. These assessments reflect our teacherly observations of how students appear to be receiving the subject matter and of what they are doing with it during class. You may already use checklists to justify your assessments and sharpen your observation skills in this regard.

English Language Arts is a wonderfully complex field of study. To assess student learning, we need a wide variety of assessment tools: How accurate is the student? How complete? How imaginative? How engaged? How inspired? How diligent? How insightful? How eloquent? How controlled? An array of performance tasks encompasses reading, writing, listening, and speaking, often overlapping, during the marking period.

I hope that performance tasks guide students toward a deeper understanding of literature and language, that they are an integral part of the learning, rather than just another form of a major unit test.

WHAT ARE THE DESIGN ELEMENTS OF A PERFORMANCE TASK?

The design of performance tasks must be standards-based. That is to say, we must begin with the question: What do we want students to *know* and be able to do when they complete these tasks.

As we look at the NCTE/IRA Standards, we find that not only do they overlap, but that single performance tasks cannot meet them on their own. It is not a matter of saying, "Here are 11 standards, so we can come up with 11 performance tasks, and check off the standards in order as we go along." Meeting the standards is an ambiguous, recursive process.

Suppose, for high school level, the Standard to be assessed is "*...learn to use word analysis and vocabulary-building techniques.*" We can begin with these essential questions:

- ◆ Product: What will the task look like when it is completed?

- ◆ Directions to the student

- ◆ Instruction: What knowledge do students need and how will they get it?

- ◆ Standards: How does this performance tasks meet this and other standards?

- ◆ Challenge Level: How will my weaker students handle this task? What parts will be difficult for them? How can I help?

- ◆ Follow-up: How will I reinforce the learning in the future?

- ◆ Scoring Guide: What will the rubric look like? What will a high-level sample look like? A mid-level sample? A low-level sample?

- ◆ Remediation: How can I help a struggling student improve?

The vocabulary Standard refers to the development of an approach to language, a habit of mind. We want students to approach new words systematically, by looking at roots, prefixes, context. We don't want them to think of every new word as an entity unrelated to other words. So, the habit of mind that we wish to instill is the habit of saying: *What do I already know about this word? How can I make an educated guess as to its meaning*? Here is one performance task design that meets this Standard:

- ◆ Product: What will the task look like when it is completed?

  Middle School students will create a poster that illustrates one Latin root, giving several examples of words that have that root. Additionally, students will compose a paragraph that uses at least three words with the given root. They will read their paragraphs aloud to the class, and explain their poster.

- ◆ Instruction: What knowledge will students need and how will they get it?

The teacher will give direct instruction about the nature of prefixes, suffixes, and roots. Given a page of sophisticated text, such as from *The New York Times*, students will highlight all unfamiliar words and the teacher will write these on the board. The teacher will then help the class to understand which of these words have Latin word roots, and will model the procedure for finding the meaning of the root as well as other words which have this root. They will illustrate the relationship between English and the Romance languages.

- ◆ Assessment: How will the task be assessed?

The teacher will develop a rubric that scores for:

- • *Meaning*: The product shows that the student clearly understands the meaning of the word root; the sentences display correct use of words having that root.

- • *Development:* The student gives a sufficient number of examples; the paragraph contains several sentences

- • *Organization:* The product displays main ideas and details in the proper sequence, showing an understanding of subordination of details to main idea

- • *Language:* The student has used word choice and sentence structure that are interesting, varied, and appropriate.

- • *Conventions:* The student has followed the rules of standard English in spelling, capitalization, punctuation, usage, and has shown care in presentation.

- ◆ Challenge Level: How will students become familiar with the criteria?

An effective technique is to have the class go over the rubric carefully, looking at the differences between the levels: What would a level 4 piece have that a level 3 piece lacks on each of the criteria?

- ◆ Follow-up: How will I reinforce the learning in the future?

The display of the posters with different word roots on them will be a visual reinforcer. Additionally, the teacher will regularly ask students to find words with Latin roots in their reading and writing, strengthening the habit of mind suggested by the Standard.

HOW DOES PERFORMANCE TASK ASSESSMENT INFLUENCE INSTRUCTION?

In the performance task above, the teacher would be instructing by modeling an approach to learning new words. The words are learned not by giving the students a list of unrelated *big words*, but by building on what the student knows about context, prefixes, suffixes, and roots.

The short-answer or unit test model is finite, and its experience is discrete from instruction: when students take the test, they are not, theoretically, learning. Rather, they are reproducing. But performance task assessment is *productive*, rather than *re*productive, in nature.

While instructing toward a performance task, you must keep the following in mind, and convey it to students:

- A performance task is completed over time, with input from various sources and through various means of communication.

- The criteria for assessment (rubrics/scoring guides) are predictable and available from the outset.

- Although you have a vision of what the task will look like when it is finished, there is room for individual interpretation. You may present models, but don't give the impression that students are limited to them.

- Completion of a performance task requires the student to integrate new knowledge with prior knowledge. This integration takes the form of decision-making, evaluation, collection of data, and other process-oriented higher order thinking skills.

- The performance task should require the expansion of the students' subject area language.

- Performance tasks usually involve communication and interaction among peers.

- In the course of completing a performance tasks, you may choose to give traditional tests to check for basic knowledge of terms, sequences, or comprehension on a literal level.

WHAT DO YOU NEED TO KNOW
ABOUT PORTFOLIO ASSESSMENT?

Much is said about portfolio assessment in a performance-based curriculum, because portfolios present a wide array of student work samples and show growth over time. Portfolios come in many flavors, formative and summative. A portfolio is a structured collection of a student's work that documents scope and progress. Portfolios have these features:

- Various *types of work* are represented, and the pieces were gathered over time. Sometimes, the student selects the works to be included, with either the teacher or the student establishing criteria for what is to be included.

- There is evidence of *process* in the form of rough drafts, lists, diagrams, notes, and other procedural devices that attest to the fact that the student *walked the walk* in producing the pieces, and that the tasks were taken seriously and completed as a result of time and thought.

- *Presentation* is important. A portfolio should be neatly organized, inviting, and representative of the student's pride in learning. Formality is one of the key ways in which a bona fide portfolio differs from a casual collection of papers jammed in a manila folder. Many portfolios contain a table of contents and have pages securely reinforced in a binder.

- The student has thought about thinking (metacognition). The portfolio should contain at least one *reflective piece* of writing, revealing the student's own assessment of her progress, challenges, learning goals, and the highlights of achievement.

Portfolios can be formally presented to an audience of peers or adjudicators. They can roll forward from one year to another, or can be limited to a particular unit of study that takes a few weeks to compile. Many teachers ask for elaborately decorated covers or boxes, and design can be a performance task in itself.

Portfolio assessment is a powerful and versatile tool that may seem daunting to the novice teacher, and many veterans are novices when it comes to portfolio assessment. Like many aspects of education reform in the last decade, portfolios have taken the profession by storm and many of us who view them at conferences feel overwhelmed by the task of supervising the collection of massive amounts of papers. Chapter 4 is devoted to portfolio management and assessment.

WHAT ARE THE TIME MANAGEMENT ISSUES INVOLVED IN USING PERFORMANCE TASKS?

Performance tasks take longer to complete than do traditional tests. Not only that, but not all students will finish at the same time, and, when we use co-operative learning groups or pairs, there is always the problem of absenteeism.

Many performance tasks also have a presentation component. Asking every student to make a presentation, even if it's only two minutes long, can obviously use an inordinate amount of time.

Although much of the work on a performance task may be done outside of class, it should not be reduced entirely to a homework assignment. Your guidance, library work, and communication with peers are essential.

When we make the transformation from traditional assessment into performance task assessment, we often hear the mantra *less is more*. Still, it is disconcerting to find time slipping away week by week and we're still doing the snow poetry unit. We may find ourselves discarding pieces of literature that were staples in the curriculum, and we wonder if we're doing the right thing.

You might want to keep the following factors in mind when considering how you can use time efficiently when doing a performance task:

- ♦ Any time students need to depend on each other for a class project, one of them will be absent at a crucial point. You need to make (or have the students make) contingency plans. Students need to be responsible on an *individual* basis for a specified part of the task, regardless of the participation level of coworkers.

- ♦ Presentations don't necessarily have to be given before the entire class. You can save time by having simultaneous presentations with smaller groups. Students can copresent, as well.

- ♦ Have students keep logs and make time management plans to chart their expected/actual progress.

- ♦ Stress the importance of not going over the time or length allotment of a task. Students who think they can *wow* you with excessive verbiage are taught an important lesson when they learn to economize.

- ♦ Remember that not everything has to be in paragraph form. Bulleted lists, labeled diagrams, a series of key words and phrases are efficient and concise ways of expressing knowledge.

- ♦ Plan for supplemental projects for early finishers if the task is worked on in class.

WHAT MAKES A PERFORMANCE TASK AUTHENTIC LEARNING?

Allan A. Glatthorn (1999) defines authentic learning as "learning that has real-life value, functions as the cornerstone of mastering that subject, and is actively constructed by the student. This is learning that is used to solve problems and complete open-ended tasks" (p. 25). You may hear other terms used synonymously with *authentic learning*: authentic assessment, performance assessment, standard-based learning, outcome-based learning, direct assessment, alternative assessment. This last term is used because performance task learning is an alternative to traditional or standardized tests.

If we want students to know what prepositional phrases are, we can have them memorize the list of prepositions and then pick out prepositional phrases in a text. That would be inauthentic because in real life no one asks us to pick out prepositional phrases from text. The activity, though it is the kind of learning that is expected in an English class, lacks real world application. But that doesn't mean that we shouldn't be teaching students what prepositions are. We need first to ask: "What is the practical application of knowing what prepositions are?" The answer is that, once we understand what prepositional phrases are, we can use them to introduce sentences, rather than introducing sentence after sentence with the subject, as novice writers always do. Prepositional phrases serve the function of providing detail of time and place. So our students will write with more variety and more detail if they develop an awareness of prepositional phrases. With that in mind, the finding of prepositional phrases in a text becomes an authentic learning experience, because it is purposeful and contextualized.

When we read literature, authentic learning occurs when we make connections, when we deepen our understanding of ourselves and of the world, when we enrich our language, and when we have had the mental travel experience that literature can provide. Literature is not only an intellectual experience, but an aesthetic one. A key piece of authenticity in the English class is developing an appreciation for the beauty of language: words, phrases, sentences, and a well-crafted essay or story.

When we ask students to learn a list of literary terms and match them to definitions on a test, we are not engaging in authentic meaning. Consider the device of foreshadowing. What is the purpose of knowing what the word *foreshadowing* means? The purpose is to make readers aware that events in a story happen not haphazardly, but in order to enrich the story. We teach the term foreshadowing so that students can better understand minor events in a story, and can make their own stories more interesting. In that sense, foreshadowing is a type of metaphor, in which we see similarities, echoes, between two events.

Questions about purpose and application illuminate the path to authentic learning.. It's easy to present a list of unrelated vocabulary words and have students look them up in a dictionary, and line them up in a matching column on Friday. We can delude ourselves into thinking that we have expanded our students' vocabulary in that way. Indeed, that method lies in the comfort zone of many students, parents, and administrators. But it is not authentic learning because we don't treat words in this way in real language. In real language, a word is used in context and can wear many hats. It has a history, subtleties, connotations, different forms. If all it took to learn new words was to look them up, write them on flashcards, and match them to definitions, we could teach toddlers to speak by giving them a list of words every day. Toddlers learn words in context, which is how we all learn throughout our lives. So we need to create a language-rich environment in which we learn new words naturally. If the words that we wish students to learn are related to each other and are applicable to an upcoming piece of writing, if we use these words ourselves in the course of instruction, if we teach fewer words and do so more thoroughly, then our students are likely to enrich their vocabularies in ways that will never happen through matching columns, flash cards, and workbooks alone.

As for literature, our assessments need to allow for the fact that the relationship between author and reader is a living thing, one that is easy to kill. Authentic assessment of literature invites the student into the world that the author has created, rather than trips him up with single-answer questions about details.

Authentic learning provides for useful strategies, allows for depth, asks students to make judgments, encourages communication, and uses real, rather than controlled, language. The editorial page of *The New York Times* is a far better source of vocabulary, sentence structure, punctuation, and reading comprehension instruction than any decontextualized, controlled list, or series of exercises.

Because these tasks are complex, *scaffolding*, is an important part of authentic learning. By this, we mean that the teacher provides structures, such as a verbal introduction to a reading piece, an outline, or a list of difficult terminology, which will establish a knowledge base. If new knowledge must *attach* to prior knowledge, then we need to provide that prior knowledge. This is where an interim short answer test can actually be useful after the fact. It can gird the student's knowledge of the book up to that point.

When we allow or require students to work on a piece until it reaches a certain level, this is known as *mastery assessment*. With traditional testing, we usually don't allow re-takes on a test: "if you didn't know the answers then," we say to the student, "we don't care if you know them now." But, in real life situations, we are often permitted to keep working on something until we get it right. Mastery assessment is not appropriate for all situations and has many obvious drawbacks, not the least of which is that it is extremely demanding on the teacher. We can make some modifications in the interest of practicality when our goal is mastery of a performance task. In portfolio assessment, students can often achieve mastery, because they can go back and rework pieces throughout the year as their skills improve.

Finally, *metacognition* (thinking about thinking) is a component of authentic learning. As students learn explicit material, they also need to track their learning styles. Did they learn by writing? by hearing? by talking? by using visuals? What is their reading rate? How can they best remember, concentrate, stay on task? Many teachers ask students to use reflective writing and learning logs as metacognitive tools.

Through authentic learning experiences, we hope that our students will develop positive attitudes about language and reading. The affective domain of learning is particularly important in an English class, where lifelong reading and love of language should be the goal.

HOW CAN YOU DEVELOP A COLLEGIAL REVIEW PROCESS?

Ideally, the entire faculty, under administrative leadership, will be on board with performance task assessment. In the absence of that, you may be able to gather a cadre of like-minded colleagues who are willing to take risks, expand their toolbox of teaching skills, and invite each other into their teaching lives. This collegiality benefits all teachers and students.

We all know the pitfalls of the isolationist *egg-crate* school, where you can teach next door to someone for 20 years and have no idea what that person is doing. Think about how fragmented the student's day is, when everyone speaks a different educational dialect. You can break down walls brick by brick. Your school may not be structured in favor of collegiality (block scheduling, teams, common planning time), but, even in the absence of these structures, you can begin by working with *one* colleague. Ask a colleague to review your performance task design. It's difficult to spot flaws in our own work. . The following questions will help you improve your plan for a particular task:

- Will the student understand the expectations? Is the wording clear and concise?

- Does the task assess the knowledge and skills that it purports to assess? Does the task assess new knowledge?

- Can the task be done in the allotted time?

- Will the students have the resources for the task?

In the best of worlds, you and your colleagues would have time to plan performance tasks, coached by an expert consultant, who models the design plan and guides you through the process. In the first year, you come to understand the nature of standards-based curriculum and authentic assessment. In that year, you and your colleagues prepare a pilot task that all of the teachers on your grade level will try. You also develop the rubric. As that first year progresses, you and your colleagues would be thinking about how to refine performance tasks that you already do, such as essays and research papers. You'll also think about how your literature, vocabulary, grammar/usage, spelling, and media work can be made more authentic. You'll begin to look at your traditional tests in a new light: not looking to discard them, but to supplement them with richer student-based work.

After the students complete the pilot task, you and your colleagues should have time not only to refine the task and rubric, but also to compare student work that receives the same grade from more than one teacher. In other words, here's your chance to learn whether your A-minus is your colleague's A-minus.

These collegial conversations are valuable on many levels. You and your colleagues don't have to walk in lockstep, but everybody benefits by knowing more about what everyone else is expecting of students.

SUMMARY

Performance task assessment (also called authentic assessment, alternative assessment, direct assessment) is a powerful mode of instruction for life-long learning. English classes are especially well suited for performance task assessment because we already do so much writing. Although traditional tests will continue to thrive, we can make our instruction more cogent when we teach students how to construct meaning out of literature and language lessons.

Once we have a clear idea of the nature of performance tasks, the next step is to understand how to assess them. As we design and use rubrics, our expectations of students come into sharper focus.

2

RUBRICS

CHAPTER OVERVIEW

This chapter tells you what you need to know about rubrics: how to design and use them both as a way to score papers accurately and consistently and as a reliable guide for the students, so that they know what is expected from a performance task as they work through it:

♦ What is a rubric and how is it used by teachers and students?

♦ What are some common pitfalls of rubric use and design?

♦ What is the most efficient rubric design for English Language Arts performance tasks?

♦ What are various methods of setting up the rubric?

♦ How do we check a rubric for flaws?

WHAT IS A RUBRIC AND HOW IS IT USED BY TEACHERS AND STUDENTS?

The word *rubric* is arcane and pretentious. I resisted it for a long time and finally capitulated. When the word *rubric* started buzzing around the academic lexicon, I, like many of you, consulted a dictionary. To my bemusement, I found that the road to rubrics traveled through a bit of fifteenth century medieval church history. Christian monks, as they meticulously copied out sections of Scripture, headed up each section with a red letter, known as a rubric. (The Latin word for red is *ruber*, as in *ruby*.) So, a rubric, etymologically, has to do with categories.

A rubric is a scoring guide: it tells the student and teacher what traits will be evaluated and presents a continuum of quality on those traits. Such a scoring guide could just as easily have been called *specs*, a term which has more *élan* than the stodgy and opaque *rubric*, but, like it or not, *rubric* is the word that we have to work with in the current climate. I'll be the first to switch over to *scoring guide* or *specs* when the term *rubric* gives way.

That said, what we refer to as a rubric is a valuable learning tool. A rubric shows the student the traits that are being evaluated and what excellence in these traits looks like. A rubric has three parts. First, it has *evaluative criteria*. These are the traits to be scored. Most English Language Arts rubrics consist of traits such as meaning (also called intent, ideas, content), development (also called substance, support, details, references, proof), organization, conventions (also called mechanics or presentation), word choice (also called diction, tone, or vocabulary), and sentence structure. Some rubrics combine word choice with sentence structure, under the heading of language or style. In addition, you may want to include something about the overall conditions of the paper: Is it neatly typed and proofread? Was it handed in on time? Does it have a proper heading? margins? spacing? Whatever is being evaluated must be stated forthrightly.

The words used to indicate quality on a continuum, such as *excellent, good, fair, unacceptable,* are the second part of your rubric. You should have either four or six levels on the quality continuum. If you have three or five, you'll find yourself huddling around that middle number, rather than making a definitive stand on the quality of a particular trait. For garden variety performance tasks, I recommend a four-station rubric. For high stakes tasks, such as final exams or exhibitions, where you might have multiple scorers, you might want a rubric that is refined to accommodate six levels of a continuum from unacceptable to excellent.

The portion of the rubric for *word choice* might look like this:

Criteria/ Levels	4 Excellent: *consistent*	3 Good: *emergent*	2 Fair: *inconsistent*	1 Unacceptable: *deficient*
Word Choice	• Is varied, interesting, appropriate • Uses figurative language			

If you define only the highest performance level and leave the rest of the boxes blank, as I've done, you have some room to write comments or give examples of weaknesses. Some teachers prefer to carry the wording throughout all of the boxes, thinking that doing so clarifies the specifications on each station.

The third part of your rubric is your *scoring strategy*. Here's where you decide how you are going to tally up your score for the total piece. You can consider each of the evaluative criteria (traits) equally, or you can work out a formula for weighting them. If you choose to use a *holistic strategy*, you will make an overall judgment and express it with a single number. If you choose a more time-consuming method, an *analytic strategy*, then you award a value to each trait, weighted or not, and calculate the result to arrive at a grade.

If the rubric is to have instructive value, the students need to have it as they work through the piece. They also need to take some responsibility to evaluate themselves and to refer to the traits as they work, just as anyone who builds something works with a set of specs. One good idea is to have the students submit the rubric along with the finished product, *with their own markings on the rubric*. They can even include a reflective piece prior to having you grade the work.

WHAT ARE SOME COMMON PITFALLS IN RUBRIC USE AND DESIGN?

You can find all manner of commercially prepared rubrics, as I present in this book, as well as rubrics sent down by state education departments. These may be useful to you, but if you are a novice, you'll need to get the feel of tailoring your own rubrics for performance tasks that you design. If you're like most novices, you'll make a number of common mistakes.

MISTAKE ONE: TOO MANY RUBRICS

When I first started using rubrics, I thought I had to have a different rubric for each task I assigned. I began each one from scratch. If the result was a paperwork overload for me, imagine what it was for my students! Gradually, I learned that the traits that I was evaluating were more or less the same for almost everything I asked my students to do. If you have too many rubrics, chances are that they are too task-specific. The idea is *not* to spell out to the students exactly what they must do to get a high grade on this particular task. If our guidelines are overly specific, then we are giving the student too much information and not allowing her to think for herself. A good rubric is general enough to apply to more than one task.

MISTAKE TWO: GENERALITIES

On the other hand, if a rubric is too broad, it might do little more than state the obvious: a trait is good because it's good. Every trait on the rubric has to be teachable and manifest. In the *word choice* segment above, the words *varied, interesting,* and *appropriate* are discrete and measurable. We aren't simply telling the students that their words have to be *well chosen* or *sophisticated*. The former is vague and circuitous; the latter, not only subjective, but specious: Not all sophisticated words are appropriate for the context. We aren't looking for a display of fancy words.

MISTAKE THREE: WORDINESS

If, in our quest for thoroughness and exactitude, we overwhelm the page with tiny lettering and full sentences, the rubric will simply not be used. Wordiness often happens when several teachers devise the rubric. It ends up having something for everybody and it looks it. I'm reminded of the maxim, "A camel is a horse designed by a committee." User-friendliness in the form of eye appeal and accessibility is paramount to a successful rubric. The *Meaning* heading for the new New York State Regents Exam in English looks like this for the three highest levels:

Quality	6 *Responses at this level:*	5 *Responses at this level:*	4 *Responses at this level:*
Meaning: the extent to which the response exhibits sound understanding, interpretation, and analysis of the task and test(s)	• Establish a controlling idea that reveals an in-depth analysis of both texts • Make insightful connections between the controlling idea, the ideas in each text, and the elements or techniques used to convey those ideas	• Establish a controlling idea that reveals a thorough understanding of both texts • Make explicit connections between the ideas in each text and the elements or techniques used to convey those ideas	• Establish a controlling idea that shows a basic understanding of the texts • Make few or superficial connections between the controlling idea, the ideas in the texts, and the elements or techniques used to convey those ideas

What you see here is the first three of six boxes running horizontally on a rubric that has five qualities running vertically. When you squish all that verbiage onto a single page, the result is quite uninviting. Of course, this particular rubric is for a high-stakes assessment, and teachers receive extensive training in its use, so it may not be as daunting as it seems. Still, we'd have to admit that even if *teachers* were to develop proficiency on such a wordy rubric, only the most conscientious of *students* would be likely to make friends with it.

Here's how we present the same information more concisely:

Quality	*6* *Responses at this* *level show:*	*5* *Responses at this* *level show:*	*4* *Responses at this* *level show:*
Meaning: does the writer understand, interpret, and analyze the task?	• In-depth analysis of task • Sharp insight into literary elements and techniques • Overt and subtle relationships between themes and details	• Good understanding of task • Some insight into literary elements and techniques • Overt relationships between themes and details	• Basic understanding of task • Basic understanding of literary elements or techniques • Basic understanding of relationships between themes and details

That's a word reduction of 33%, and we've also put the language into the vernacular, which brings us into the next mistake.

MISTAKE FOUR: JARGON

All professionals use esoteric language, but, just as one of our standards is to teach students how to suit their language to the audience, we have to suit ours to theirs. This means eschewing such phrases as "the extent to which the response exhibits direction, shape, and coherence" in favor of "the extent to which the writing follows an outline." It's easy to slip into ed-speak, but we lose our audience when we do so. Fortunately, vernacular language takes up less space than jargon and makes for a roomier page.

There's a difference between rubrics created for large-scale, standardized assessments, such as state or national exams, and those created for classroom use. For the former, there will be more than one rater. The more finely calibrated the scale, the higher the likelihood of between-rater agreement (Popham, 1997). Such rubrics are for teacher, not student, use. We can always present a *translated* vernacular version of these rubrics, so that students can practice. For garden-variety classroom rubrics, where only one teacher will be assessing the task, a four point rubric written in simple language is most likely to be used as a guide by students.

In "What's Wrong and What's Right with Rubrics," James Popham sums up the choices: "…in almost all instances, lengthy rubrics probably can be reduced to succinct but far more useful versions for classroom instruction. Such abbreviated rubrics can still capture the key evaluative criteria needed to judge students' responses. Lengthy rubrics, in contrast, will gather dust" (1997, p. 74).

WHAT IS THE MOST EFFICIENT RUBRIC DESIGN FOR ENGLISH LANGUAGE ARTS PERFORMANCE TASKS?

Popham refers to rubrics as "instructional illuminators." So, a rubric should be simple to use, clear, and relevant not only to this particular task, but to the larger issues of thinking in the subject area. It is a consummation devoutly to be wished that the student come to internalize knowledge about quality traits so that they no longer need to consult the specs. For this to happen, we need to present rubrics that have consistent structure and language.

Let's consider a four-point rubric (*excellent, good, fair, unacceptable*) on five traits. We'll look at rubric designs for the two kinds of performance tasks described in Chapter 1: *product* (written and physical) and *behavior* (structured and spontaneous.)

RUBRIC FOR A WRITTEN OR PHYSICAL PRODUCT

MEANING (ALSO CALLED INTENT, IDEAS, CONTENT)

This, the first column, evaluates the extent to which the student did what was asked for. One of our biggest frustrations about the way our students write is that they didn't give us what we asked for. Instead of addressing a thematic question, they summarized. Instead of tracing character development, they summarized. Instead of analyzing literary devices, they summarized. So, *job one* is to stay focused. The task will use key verbs of higher order thinking, such as *interpret, analyze, compare/contrast, develop, design, persuade, defend, critique,* and *evaluate.* The key verb should then appear in the rubric. Key adjectives are *in-depth, insightful,* and *perceptive.* If the task involves showing understanding of reading material, then the writer needs to express an understanding of the author's intent: the tone and purpose. If the student misinterpreted the question, lapsed into summary, or stayed at a superficial level of analysis, the lower level of the continuum would indicate these weaknesses.

DEVELOPMENT (ALSO CALLED SUBSTANCE, SUPPORT, DETAILS, REFERENCES, PROOF)

This part of the rubric evaluates the extent to which the writer provided sufficient relevant and specific information. Key nouns that you can use here are *reasons, examples, descriptions, statistics, quotations,* and *references.* Key adjectives are *various, fully, thorough, relevant focused,* and *multifaceted.* If the writer has strayed from the topic and included irrelevancies and redundancies, the lower levels of the continuum would be the place to indicate these weaknesses.

Padding, the inclusion of deliberately wordy information used to give the illusion of substance, can be indicated here or under the *meaning* heading.

ORGANIZATION (ALSO CALLED STRUCTURE, ORDER, SEQUENCING)

This part of the rubric evaluates the extent to which the piece has structure, shape, logical flow, and transition. It takes into account the presence of paragraphing, topic sentences, transition, introduction, and conclusion. Key nouns: order, logic, progression, and transition. Key verbs: lead, progress, link, connect, and follow. Structural flaws, such as the absence of topic sentences, and other such *qualities of chaos* as nonsequiturs, lack of paragraphing, and absence of the expected parts of a writing piece would be noted in the lower ranges.

WORD CHOICE (ALSO CALLED DICTION, STYLE, TONE, VOICE, FLUENCY, VOCABULARY, OR LANGUAGE)

This part of the rubric evaluates the extent to which the piece shows control over diction and sentence structure, appropriateness of tone, varied and interesting vocabulary, and use of figurative language. Here is where we comment on whether sentence after sentence begins with the subject, creating a choppy effect. Here also, is where skilled use of punctuation to achieve rhythm, ease of reading, conciseness and control come in. We are also looking for language variety: ability to use synonyms where appropriate, ability to deploy a variety of punctuation marks, and ability to manage many different kinds of grammatical structures. We're also looking for refinements and control of long sentences: parallel structure, subordination, and contrasting elements. In terms of vocabulary, we're evaluating for appropriateness. Does the student understand when to use technical terms and when to use the vernacular? Does he use elevated Latin- and Greek-based words as well as strong Anglo Saxon words? Does it look as though this student is reaching out for new words? Do we see words that we've taught in class? Do we see literary terms? Is the figurative language fresh, or is it trite? Has the student tried using allusion? Is there a pithy title?

Word Choice is a comprehensive category. I'm tempted to break it in two: vocabulary and sentence structure. The only thing that keeps me from doing so is that I don't want my rubric to exceed one page, and I'm adhering to the advice of experts that a serviceable rubric should be limited to five criteria.

This is also where we consider the sense of audience. Has the student used slang in a formal essay? Has she used a dry tone where the piece is meant to amuse? Does she sound stuffy or stilted? Some students overdo this in their efforts to sound poetic, and they can sound cloying, like someone with too much perfume.

We should encourage students to use figurative language, humor, irony, allusion, and other gems of language that we point out in the literature that we teach.

Word choice also includes the qualities of conciseness and vigor. Here is where we indicate that we find awkward phrasing, passive voice, and muddiness. We're noting sentences choked with word weeds, ramblers, overstatements, and empty statements.

Though there is a black line on the rubric to distinguish one evaluative criterion from its neighbor, the traits bleed into each other. Many of the atrocities described in the *word choice* category also apply to *conventions*. When it comes to evaluating language it can be difficult to discriminate between a grammatical error and a stylistic one. What's grammatically perfect may be stylistically dead. Perhaps the best adjective to describe what we're looking for in word choice is *robust*. Robust language is strong, healthy, vivid, intense, and clear.

CONVENTIONS (ALSO CALLED MECHANICS OR PRESENTATION)

This part of the rubric evaluates the extent to which the student uses the correct protocols of Standard Written English. That includes spelling, punctuation, capitalization, subject/verb agreement, correct verb forms, pronoun/antecedent agreement, correct pronoun case and number, and other such matters. It also includes presentation: that the piece is handed in on time, on the proper type of paper, stapled or clipped as specified, bearing the proper heading, with regulation fonts, spacing, and margins. It would also include proper documentation techniques on a research paper.

PHYSICAL PRODUCT

The above descriptions apply to writing tasks, but they can be easily adapted to other performance tasks. For a physical product, such as a decorated box of props or a book cover design, you could replace *development* with *design* and include such visual aspects as color choice, dominant image, secondary images, and symbolism. Most physical products do have some verbal component, even if it's just a brief explanation, given orally or written on an index card. A physical product in an English class has much in common with a work of advertising, where the language is succinct and pithy. Often, the project is humorous in tone.

A physical product can easily miss the mark where *meaning* is concerned. Its literary value can be lost to the intricacy of the artwork. If students are making a model of the Globe Theater, there should be a verbal component wherein they bring in the impact of design on performance. They could talk about the implications of having no curtain, or no amplification. They could note that, in Shakespearean plays, the actor would often turn himself around during monologues, playing to all sides of the house. Or, they could point out several examples of the bawdy lines that were pitched to the groundlings, as opposed to the lofty speeches written to please the monarch. The task has to be carefully designed so that English Language Arts standards are met, which is why we *begin* performance task design with the standards. Whether it be a classroom poster or a soundtrack, *meaning*, in terms of the standards, is still foremost: Did the student meet the specs? Were the specs in line with English Language Arts standards?

You may combine the categories of organization and development for a physical product. Everything assembled to convey meaning has to have some schematic structure. Is there logical subordination of details to main idea? Does the piece consist of multiple elements, such as a decorated props box? Are the items numbered, clustered, labeled, presented in some order?

Lastly, for *conventions*, presentation can be called *workmanship* or *detailing*. The product can't be displayed if it has gross errors, is messy, or unsturdy.

A Word on Interdisciplinary Projects

The headings of Meaning, Development, Organization, Language, and Conventions cover the territory that you need to assess, as well as to teach, in written and physical products in English class. With the support of colleagues, they can help you achieve consistency of language within the English department. It's also worth trying to interest your colleagues in the other disciplines to use this terminology as well. In writing a lab report, for example, these headings apply, as they do for any social studies report. As we've seen, we have many synonyms, and, although students should develop flexibility, they shouldn't have the sense that it's an altogether different ball game from one class to the next. Science teachers don't necessarily care about literary techniques in their lab reports, but they do have a word choice component: they are looking for proper terminology and concise wording. If the wording is not focused, then the message isn't clear, and if the message isn't clear, then the science teacher doesn't know if the student understands the meaning.

Rubrics for Structured or Spontaneous Behavior

Panel discussions, prepared speeches, dramatic readings, rehearsed scripted scenes, and planned interviews are examples of performance tasks for which we assess structured behavior.

When assessing behavior, we can combine *meaning and development* as the first criterion: Did the students stay focused on the task? Unskilled or unprepared students will drift away from the topic or lapse into repetition. If the performance is based on scripted material, the meaning and development would be manifest in how the lines are delivered to convey meaning.

Whether organization is an appropriate heading for a behavioral task depends on the extent to which the student had to do the organizing. Organization is not a factor in a dramatic reading or scripted scene, but it is definitely a factor in a planned interview.

In assessing a behavioral task, I prefer the term *language use* to *word choice*. Language use refers not only to vocabulary level, but also to habits of speech: Is the style free of word weeds such as *like, ya know, um*? Is the delivery audible and distinct? If the student is explaining something in her own words, is she using proper terminology or relying on lazy fillers, such as *the thingy* and *the whatsis*. The rules for spoken English are more relaxed than those for Standard Written English, but a reasonable level of colloquial English usage would be expected.

The *conventions* of a behavioral task are the conventions of speaking etiquette: eye contact, a businesslike posture, a facial expression that shows interest and undivided attention to other speakers, speaking in turn, showing enthusiasm.

For assessment of spontaneous behavior, you need a different kind of rubric. By spontaneous behavior, we mean habits of classroom citizenship, which can also be called class participation or attitude. We shouldn't overlook this aspect of performance even though it may seem elusive. Years ago, all that counted were percentages on a test. But that way of thinking reduces education to a *factory model*. Today, we know that assessment can be more sophisticated and can be based on a variety of factors. A test or a task will never cover all the territory of what a student knows and can do. That is why we should include spontaneous behavior that does, or does not, manifest learning.

How do you know that a student takes learning seriously and is an active member of your class? Attitude and effort usually play a part, especially in the lower grades, in overall assessment. Behaviors such as handing work in on time, asking appropriate questions, offering responses, offering to read aloud, staying on task, setting a good example, having good attendance, being willing to lead, and seeking assistance are all observable signs that a student is reaching out to learn in your class.

In addition to these public behaviors are personal behaviors (habits of mind), such as keeping an organized notebook, writing due dates in a daily planner, coming to class on time and prepared with materials, and making up work missed during absences. All of these behaviors fall under the heading of *conscientious work habits*. When we consider how important such behaviors are in the workplace, we see the value of including them in classroom assessment. Qualities such as persistence, willingness to listen to others, willingness to take intellectual risks, and meticulousness and attention to detail are all behaviors that we can assess from time to time.

Finally, we can observe and assess certain metacognitive habits. Does the student show an interest in learning from your comments and corrections? Is he sincere about improving his skills, or does he care only about the grade? When he writes a reflective piece, does he show insight into his learning style? Does he have an awareness of his strengths and weaknesses? Does he follow up on suggestions for improvement?

SUMMARY

A sturdy structure for an English Language Arts rubric evaluates for meaning, development, organization, word choice, and conventions. For ordinary classroom assessments, a four-level rubric (excellent, good, fair, unacceptable) will suffice. We will probably refine the rubric to six levels if there is to be more than one reader on a high stakes test. We can adapt the basic criteria to other types of performance tasks, such as physical projects or dramatic presentations. Additionally, we can have a rubric that assesses for spontaneous behavior, the habits of mind that students exhibit and that are a part of their learning. Rubrics are most effective when they are user friendly, predictable, and concise.

WHAT ARE VARIOUS METHODS FOR SETTING UP THE RUBRIC?

You can set up your rubric with *boxes going across* the page, or you can work with a *checklist going down* the page. You can also combine these two formats. Several formats are presented here because some teachers prefer one over another.

FORMAT ONE: BOXES

SCORING GUIDE: WRITTEN TASK

Criteria/ Levels	Excellent: *consistent*	Good: *emergent*	Fair: *inconsistent*	Unacceptable: *deficient*
Meaning	• Sharp focus on the question • Insight, depth			• Missing the point of the question • Stating the obvious
Development	• Reasons, examples, explanations • Strong paragraph structure			• Lacking support • Redundant • Irrelevant • Too brief or too long
Organization	• All components present • Strong transitions • Coherence			• Lacking transition
Word Choice	• Varied, interesting, appropriate vocabulary/sentence structure • Figurative language • Clarity • Conciseness			• Flat language • Wordiness • Incoherent sentences
Conventions	• Free of errors • Careful proofreading • Careful presentation			• Many errors in basic usage • Not proofread • Careless presentation

FORMAT TWO: CHECKLIST

SCORING GUIDE: WRITTEN TASK

With a few minor adjustments on the wording, the same rubric could be set up vertically.

- **Meaning:** The writer maintains a sharp focus; content shows insight and depth.

  4. _____

  3. _____

  2. _____

  1. _____

- **Development:** The writer gives sufficient reasons, examples, descriptions, or explanations to fully support key points.

  4. _____

  3. _____

  2. _____

  1. _____

- **Organization:** The writer includes all component parts: introduction, well-developed paragraphs with transitions, conclusion. The piece is coherent, with all sentences relevant and presented in a logical sequence.

  4. _____

  3. _____

  2. _____

  1. _____

- **Word Choice:** The writer uses vocabulary and sentence structure which are varied, interesting, and appropriate. The writer uses figurative language effectively. Sentences are clear and concise.

  4. _____

  3. _____

  2. _____

  1. _____

♦ **Conventions:** The writer shows full control of spelling, capitalization, punctuation, and usage. The presentation is neat and conforms to specifications.

4. _____

3. _____

2. _____

1. _____

The advantage of the above style is that you have more room to write comments that justify your checkmarks or refer the student to specific segments of the piece. Also, you may prefer the full sentence, stipulating what you require at the level of excellence, as opposed to the brevity of words that is necessary in the box rubric. The box rubric seems to be favored for standardized tests, where raters will not be making comments that the students will see.

FORMAT THREE: COMBINED

SCORING GUIDE: WRITTEN TASK

The following rubric combines these two forms:

Scoring Guide	4	3	2	1
Meaning: Interpreting the task • Doing exactly what the task asks for _____ • Staying focused _____ • Showing depth and insight _____				

Scoring Guide	4	3	2	1
Development: Providing sufficient support • Explanations and detail _____ • Examples and reasons _____ • Facts and figures _____				

Scoring Guide	4	3	2	1
Organization: Having a logical sequence • Introduction _____ • Well-developed paragraphs with topic sentences _____ • Transition _____ • Conclusion _____ • Coherence (all pieces are related) _____				

Scoring Guide	4	3	2	1
Word Choice: Interesting vocabulary and sentence structure • Variety _____ • Appropriateness _____ • Figurative language _____ • Clarity and conciseness _____				

Scoring Guide	4	3	2	1
Conventions: Correctness and presentation • Spelling _____ • Capitalization _____ • Punctuation _____ • Grammar usage _____ • Attractive and careful presentation _____				

It takes a little while to get used to grading against a rubric. You will tailor the style and content of your rubrics to fit your thinking and teaching style. Using a rubric eliminates the quandary of not knowing what to say on a student's paper. Although you can certainly write additional comments, using a rubric saves you time in the long run.

These rubrics assume equal value for all criteria. You can manipulate the value of a given criterion for a given task; sometimes, you place great value on language use, other times, on organization.

CHECKING YOUR RUBRIC FOR FLAWS

You won't really know if your rubric is flawed until you start to use it, and then the flaws will jump out at you like a splash of cold water and you'll wonder how you could have missed them. As with proofreading, another pair of eyes is likely to spot glaring errors that you would miss. That is why the following questions are best answered by colleagues, rather than by you:

♦ Is every skill teachable and demonstrable?

♦ Does the rubric reflect instruction?

♦ Is it overladen with jargon? Does it speak in a language style that students will understand?

♦ Does it cover the overarching thinking skills of the task, rather than its *specifics?*

♦ Will the student be a better thinker as a result of it?

♦ Is it as concise as it can possibly be?

♦ Is it not more than one page, with typeface large enough to read easily?

SUMMARY

A rubric is successful if it sharpens the task and its expectations without being overly directive. Because you and your students need to work hand in glove with the rubric, it needs to be a part of instruction from start to finish, not an afterthought. The rubric should tell the student what the difference is between work that is acceptable and that which is excellent.

As we design rubrics, we focus on content and skills, and that brings us into state and national learning standards: what do we want our students to know and be able to do?

Those concepts and competencies are enumerated by state education departments as well as by the NCTE/IRA (National Council of Teachers of English/International Reading Association).

A final thought: Don't feel that you have to use a rubric for everything that you grade. As with any skill, learning how to make and use rubrics is a clumsy and recursive process which will become more natural with practice. Simplicity of design will get you further than a mania for detail. Start small, work with colleagues, and keep revising.

3

ENGLISH LANGUAGE ARTS STANDARDS

CHAPTER OVERVIEW

This chapter tells you what you need to know about the Standards at state and national levels.

 ♦ What is the theory behind the Standards?

 ♦ What are the Standards for English Language Arts?

 ♦ What are the instructional implications of the Standards?

 ♦ NCTE/IRA Standards phrased as questions

 ♦ What role does grammar instruction play in the Standards?

WHAT IS THE THEORY BEHIND THE STANDARDS?

The term *Standards* when used in an educational context, refers to a list of statements that describe the concepts and competencies that students should have in their grasp at the end of their schooling. *Standards* is capitalized when referring to a designated list, whether that be the list of Standards set forth by a state education department, or the list that comes from the National Council of Teachers of English/International Reading Association (NCTE/IRA). In this book, the Standards are a distillation of both, expressed in accessible language.

A little history: In the 1970s *behavioral objectives* were all the rage. These were highly targeted statements that began with the words: *Given_____, the student will be able to....* An action verb followed, delineating some measurable "behavior": *write, list, answer a certain number of questions*, and so on. Perhaps it was the militaristic nature of behavioral objectives, or maybe it was that not everything worth learning is quite so quantifiable, that caused the term to become laughable after a while. The next wave (late 1970s) was something called *basic competency*, a term that became associated with having mediocrity as a goal. The intent was no different from our goals of today: to have high school graduates demonstrate a certain level of skills and knowledge. Trouble was, that level was rather low.

When the education reform movement began in the mid 1980s, in response to the notorious *A Nation at Risk* report, the term of choice to describe what students should know and be able to do was *learning outcomes* or *outcome-based education*. But because education is such a politically incendiary issue, the term *outcome* came to be disdained by certain influential social critics. *Outcome-based education*, for those who wonder what happened to it, fell into undeserved disrepute: it was associated with the demise of all that is good and holy: the Friday spelling test, the 45-minute essay, the matching column, and the darling of the (imaginary) golden years of American education, the sentence diagram. The term *outcome* became too closely associated with the controversial philosophy of *whole language*, and, rather than slow down the process of education reform by constantly refuting this misconception, those who speak and write about education replaced the O-word with the word *standard*. Standards are then subdivided into content standards, performance standards, and opportunity-to-learn standards (OTLs).

What, then, are the differences, if any, among the words *objective, competency, outcome,* and *standard?* Accordingly, what is it about our goal-making strategies that causes us to have to reinvent the wheel every 10 years? Do we ever reach any of our goals, or do we just keep renaming the whole enterprise?

I contend that objectives, competencies, outcomes, and standards all refer to goals, and that these terms have given way to others because purists, in their inflexibility and messianic zeal, have tangled themselves in their own language traps. For instance, Nel Noddings (1997) quotes the following statement that Wisconsin's Gov. Tommy Thompson proposed as a Standard at the fourth grade level: "Show a basic understanding of the role played by religion and civic values in the history of Wisconsin and the nation, and describe how that role is similar to, or different from, that role in an ancient civilization and a feudal society in Europe or China" (p. 189). This absurd statement illustrates what often happens in educational parlance.

The terminology may change, but the concept remains. We've always been talking about establishing goals. We want students to have certain knowledge and skills by the time they receive their diplomas. Standards, then, are learning outcomes. The difference between a Standard and a benchmark is the difference between commencement objectives and grade level objectives. The Standard represents the overall destination; the benchmarks are stops (checkpoints) along the way.

In New Jersey, for example, the English Language Arts Standards assert four basic assumptions:

1. Language use is an active process of constructing meaning.

2. Language develops in a social context.

3. Language ability increases in complexity if language is used in increasingly complex ways.

4. Learners achieve language arts literacy not by adding skills one-by-one to their repertoire, but rather by using and exploring language in its many dimensions.

The standards, or learning goals, for English Language Arts are usually presented as a list of discrete skills, but these skills are overlapping and interdependent. We need to regard the standards as a whole. They are about instilling an educated approach to language, rather than *covering* a set body of material. Teaching the standards means teaching higher order thinking: making judgments, evaluating information, developing a broad language repertoire, becoming an efficient and careful reader, distinguishing the nuances of language, adjusting one's communication style to the situation and audience. The standards have to do with habits of mind: considering the perspective of a writer, looking for multiple meanings, having a willingness to reread, being able to adjust one's reading rate, knowing what to expect from a particular genre.

WHAT ARE THE STANDARDS FOR ENGLISH LANGUAGE ARTS?

As you might expect, the Standards are not standardized in their language across state lines. They vary in layout and terminology. What are called *Cumulative Progress Indicators* in one state may be called *Benchmarks* in another, and *Performance Indicators* in yet another. One state refers to *credibility* in the same context that another refers to *perspective*. In New York, one of the Standards under the *literary response and expression* category states: "…evaluate literary merit based on an understanding of the genre and the literary elements." In New Jersey, a corresponding Standard is worded as "…understand the study of literature and theories of literary criticism." Within states, and even within districts, what are referred to as *linked passages* is called *comparative literature* somewhere else, and *controlling idea* somewhere else.

The closest we get to having national standards is this list, set forth by the NCTE/IRA (National Council of Teachers of English/ International Reading Association). These Standards have been described as comprehensive by some; incomprehensible, by others:

1. Students read a wide range of print and nonprint texts to build an understanding of texts, of themselves, and of the cultures of the

United States and the world; to acquire new information; to respond to the needs and demands of society and the workplace; and for personal fulfillment. Among these texts are fiction and nonfiction, classic and contemporary works.

2. Students read a wide range of literature from many periods and in many genres to build an understanding of the many dimensions (e.g., philosophical, ethical, aesthetic) of human experience.

3. Students apply a wide range of strategies to comprehend, interpret, evaluate, and appreciate texts. They draw on their prior experience, their interactions with other readers and writers, their knowledge of word meaning and other texts, their word identification strategies, and their understanding of textual features (e.g., sound-letter correspondence, sentence structure, context, graphics).

4. Students adjust their use of spoken, written and visual language (e.g., conventions, style, vocabulary) to communicate effectively with a variety of audiences and for different purposes.

5. Students employ a wide range of strategies as they write and use different writing process elements appropriately to communicate with different audiences for a variety of purposes.

6. Students apply knowledge of language structure, language conventions (e.g., spelling and punctuation), media techniques, figurative language and genre to create, critique, and discuss print and non-print texts.

7. Students conduct research on issues and interests by generating ideas and questions, and by posing problems. They gather, evaluate, and synthesize data from a variety of sources (e.g., print and nonprint texts, artifacts, people) to communicate their discoveries in ways that suit their purpose and audience.

8. Students use a variety of technological and informational resources (e.g., libraries, databases, computer networks, video) to gather and synthesize information and to create and communicate knowledge.

9. Students develop an understanding of and respect for diversity in language use, patterns, and dialects across cultures, ethnic groups, geographic regions, and social roles.

10. Students whose first language is not English make use of their first language to develop competency in the English language and to develop understanding of content across the curriculum.

11. Students participate as knowledgeable, reflective, creative, and critical members of a variety of literacy communities.

As we read through this list, clearly we need handier language. The editors of *Literary Cavalcade*, a national magazine published by Scholastic, have compiled a list summarizing the standards from California, Colorado, Florida, Georgia, Illinois, Indiana, Missouri, New Jersey, New York, and Texas, as well as the above NCTE/IRA Standards. Figure 3.1 presents standards in accessible, vernacular language on the left side. The right side lists some types of performance tasks that correspond to these standards.

WHAT ARE THE INSTRUCTIONAL IMPLICATIONS OF THE STANDARDS?

When we put the Standards into plain English, we can see that the goal is to have students engage in higher-level thinking that will serve them across the disciplines. The Standards require active learning with plenty of communication among peers. The Standards are not achieved through teacher talk, but through an atmosphere that promotes student talk. The teacher's role is not merely to disseminate information and evaluate performance, but to foster, model, and preside over a rich and complex learning environment.

Also clear is the contextual, overlapping, and recursive nature of the Standards. After we've completed a performance task that focuses on a particular Standard, we don't then just make a checkmark and consider that Standard *done*. Nor do we divvy up the list of Standards and say "ninth grade does the first five, tenth grade does six through ten," and so on.

The Standards are designed K-12 and, in many ways, represent more of a philosophy than a prescription, which is probably how they differ from *behavioral objectives*. They are not finite, and that is how they differ from *basic competencies*.

Many of the Standards are more about the *how* of learning, than about the *what*: they represent thinking strategies, rather than a body of knowledge. They allow for individual learning styles and invite reflection.

The performance tasks in this book that deal with poetry, for example, don't focus on the content of particular poems. Rather, they teach students how to *unwrap* any poem, how to use prior knowledge to approach complex language.

The Standards are a lens through which we view the wide scope of English Language Arts instruction. Language is our most complex achievement. Assessing competencies in anything so broad demands a variety of performance tasks. Some, such as research papers and portfolios, span weeks or months. Others, such

(Text continues on page 45.)

FIGURE 3.1. STANDARDS AND
CORRESPONDING PERFORMANCE TASKS

Standard	Types of Performance Tasks: Students demonstrate competence in these Standards when they…
1. Learn to use word analysis and vocabulary-building techniques	• Analyze contextual cues • Present "word stories," the etymological history of a word • Find synonyms and perceive distinctions between them • See the relationship between words in English and words in other Latinate languages • Organize word lists according to roots, prefixes, suffixes • Keep a personal word journal • Use and understand idioms, literal/figurative language, denotation, and connotation • Play word games; do crossword puzzles
2. Apply reading strategies, including both literal and inferential comprehension skills, to improve understanding of written works	• Take notes, summarize, paraphrase, outline • Extract salient information from the text • Perceive multiple levels of meaning • Be able to skim, scan, and review reading material • Read a variety of texts for a variety of purposes • Adjust reading rate to suit the text and purpose • Keep a reader response journal • Participate in a literary discussion group
3. Use headings, captions, pictures, and other textual clues to enhance understanding	• Use scanning techniques to get a gist of reading material before reading • Develop the habit of reading editor's notes, side notes, footnotes, captions • Pay attention to graphics to enhance and clarify meaning

Standard	***Types of Performance Tasks:*** *Students demonstrate competence in these Standards when they…*
4. Interpret tables, graphs, charts, maps	• Incorporate tables, graphs, charts, maps in their own writing • Translate such information into their own words • Develop the habit of reading both the text and the graphic information
5. Identify the distinct qualities of literary genres	• Write original pieces in various genres • Predict the features of a piece which is presented as a particular genre • Read a variety of genres • Translate literature from one genre to another • Compile thematic anthologies consisting of various genres • Write and/or recognize parodies of particular genres
6. Identify the distinct qualities of subgenres	• List and identify subgenres of a particular genre, e.g., types of mystery stories: *the detective story, the whodunit, the gothic mystery,* etc. • Identify the distinguishing characteristics and nuances of a subgenre
7. Understand how literary elements and techniques convey meaning and add nuance and beauty to a written work	• Write original pieces, using literary techniques • Distinguish between figurative and literal language • Read a wide variety of works of literary merit • Identify poetic elements in prose as well as poetry • Distinguish between literary and nonliterary writing
8. Understand and use the terminology of literary criticism	• Read reviews of books, film, art, and music, noting the features of this genre • Establish criteria for judging a work of literature • Justify one's opinion about the quality of a work of literature

Standard	*Types of Performance Tasks:* *Students demonstrate competence in these Standards when they...*
9. Read and understand literature of various cultures and eras	• Compile anthologies of multicultural literature on a particular theme • Discern aspects of life which are universal to all cultures • Discern aspects of life which are indigenous to specific cultures • Develop interdisciplinary awareness of the links between English and social studies • Read complete works as well as abridgments, excerpts, adaptations and film versions of literary classics
10. Research Skills: Identify, organize, analyze, and use information from various sources	• Write various types of research papers • Write reports and feature articles • Paraphrase, giving credit to the source Compose a formal bibliography or list of works cited • Use modern documentation techniques • Compile annotated bibliographies on a particular subject • Solve problems, using research from various sources • Have library scavenger hunts
11. Write for a variety of purposes and audiences	• Express the same message in different ways, for different audiences • Write for real audiences, outside of school: *letters to the editor, proposals, petitions, memos, letters to authors,* etc. • Adjust tone and point of view to suit the audience and situation

Standard	*Types of Performance Tasks:* *Students demonstrate competence in these Standards when they...*
12. Use the writing process effectively	• Use pre-writing strategies • Understand that time management skills are part of the writing process • Use editing and peer review strategies • Use revision strategies effectively • Share one's writing with others • Respond to the writing of others • Support interpretations, decisions, assertions • Use a variety of organizational patterns • Use proofreading skills effectively
13. Write in a variety of genres	• Express versions of the same idea in the form of several genres • Write parodies • Write in the nonfiction genres: *business reports, advertising, reviews, sportswriting,* etc. • Write sequels, prequels and "lost chapters" mimicking the style of the author
14. Understand and apply the concept of voice	• Write personal journals in one's own voice • Write personal journals, adopting the voice of fictitious or historical characters • Read and write humorous monologues
15. Understand and apply the concept of tone	• Recognize, read and write satire • Distinguish between denotation and connotation • Express the same message in different tones
16. Understand the importance of sensory detail in a written work	• Identify sensory detail in literature • Write descriptions that are rich in sensory detail • Identify sensory detail in sports writing and music reviews

Standard	Types of Performance Tasks: Students demonstrate competence in these Standards when they...
17. Use correct grammar, spelling, punctuation, capitalization, and structure	• Proofread and edit own drafts • Proofread and edit drafts written by others • Develop a personal spelling demons list • Distinguish between active and passive voice and use these styles effectively • Assist in the development of a school wide style sheet • Develop the habit of using a reference guide
18. Listen effectively in a variety of situations	• Know and use one's own best listening comprehension strategies • Participate in formal interviews • Practice effective listening habits: *eye contact, note-taking, asking questions,* etc. • Develop strategies to screen out distractions • Develop strategies to focus on key concepts
19. Speak effectively in a variety of situations	• Participate in formal interviews, panel discussions, planned and extemporaneous presentations of various lengths • View and critique oneself on videotape Interpret body language cues • Develop both a formal and an informal style of speech
20. Use effective viewing strategies for nonprint media	• Understand the relationship between graphic and text • Interpret overt and subtle visual symbols • Recognize foreshadowing in film • Develop cultural literacy in the world of film: *understand why certain films have landmark significance; identify hallmark scenes, know the significant contributions of various directors*

as in-class essays, take one period to complete. Some Standards, by their very nature, cannot be accomplished by the individual alone, but must be accomplished through communication with others. The Standards promote communication outside the classroom, with people of different generations, among people of different cultures.

Teaching to the Standards does involve creating a positive classroom climate and that, in turn, is dependent on a positive school wide climate. This implies collegiality, and collegiality is unlikely to flourish without administrative support and funding. Linda Darling-Hammond and Beverly Falk (1997) assert that "...raising standards for students so that they learn what they need to know requires raising standards for the system, so that it provides the kinds of teaching and school settings students need in order to learn" (p. 194).

WHAT ROLE DOES GRAMMAR INSTRUCTION PLAY IN THE STANDARDS?

In this book, the terms *grammar* and *syntax* are used interchangeably. At the outset, we will establish the distinction between *grammar/syntax* and *usage* (aka *mechanics, conventions*). By *grammar*, I mean the understanding of *the language of the language*. Students need to know what the following instruction means:

> Sharpen your focus by getting more specific with your nouns. Eliminate superfluous modifiers. Vary your sentence structure by beginning some sentences with prepositional phrases instead of with the subject. Your writing will be more interesting and complex if you incorporate more subordinate clauses, but don't allow a subordinate clause to stand as a complete sentence.

Simply put, we can't speak coherently about language unless we have the terminology. To the extent that having an understanding of grammatical concepts enables us to communicate about language, we need to understand those concepts. These concepts should be embedded in performance tasks: Students should have a way of *using* what they learn about grammar. Thus, grammar instruction is a means to an end and the end is clear, concise, interesting, appropriate language.

Various terms refer to the set of do's and don'ts in Standard English. *Conventions, usage,* and *mechanics* are the terms we use to denote the rules. We know that such matters are best taught in context, rather than as isolated skills.

Even the most casual discussion of grammar engages us in a confusing array of nomenclature. Half the frustration of teaching (and learning) grammar is that someone is always laying on new names for a concept that already had a confusing name: a participial adjective is now being called a gerundive; a main clause may be called a dependent clause. Adding to that frustration is the fact that many English teachers, untrained as grammarians, shy away from grammar instruction altogether, thinking that *the writing process* takes care of it all.

Knowing that the world will never speak a unified language of grammar, we can try to have an agreed-upon lexicon in-house, but there's not much we can do about grammarians, linguists, and editors simply having different terms for the same things. What's a comma splice to one is called a run-on to another, a comma blunder to another, and a fused sentence to still another. There's not much we can do about that except to consider it part of the wonderful profusion of words that populate the English language.

That said, grammar instruction, whether it be prescriptive (do's and don'ts) or rhetorical (knowing the language of the language), should undergird the Standards. What, then, should students know and be able to do in terms of grammar? The Assembly of Teachers of English Grammar (ATEG), an affiliate of the National Council of Teachers of English, is in the process of writing a scope and sequence for grammar instruction. Realize that these skills and concepts should not be taught separately, but integrated into the other Standards, *so that students will…*

- ◆ Speak and write comfortably in standard English, with an awareness of the appropriateness of dialect and nonstandard idiom in some situations.

- ◆ Be conversant in the grammatical structure of a text, show knowledge of the relationship between meaning and grammar, and how changes in one effect changes in the other.

- ◆ Understand that language changes across time, from region to region, and in various social situations. Students will appreciate and value linguistic variations and will understand the nature of dialect-based prejudices.

- ◆ Appreciate the fact that cultural variations and dialect contribute to our nation's heritage and are to be valued in terms of expressive capacity, logical structure, and beauty.

Our job as English teachers is to make students secure in their use of Standard English. Lack of education in the vagaries of Standard English renders a speaker/writer insecure. The secure speaker/writer is able to recognize when Standard English prescriptives are inappropriate to the context.

There is a subtle but significant distinction among the terms *objectives, competencies,* and *standards.* Standards are expressed differently by different states and bureaus, but, once we put them into plain English, we can develop performance tasks to assess them and we can see how they are the guiding lights of instruction. The Standards are presented in the form of a numbered list, as if they are discrete skills to be mastered one at a time. But they are in fact highly inter-connected and achieved cumulatively, over the course of many years.

THE STANDARDS PHRASED AS QUESTIONS

Here are the NCTE/IRA Standards phrased as questions:

- ◆ Can you analyze, interpret, evaluate what you hear and read?

- ◆ Can you sort out the main ideas from the supportive details?

- ◆ Can you figure out the perspective of a particular writer/speaker?

- ◆ Can you express yourself clearly, concisely, correctly?

- ◆ Can you extract key points from what you read/hear?

- ◆ Can you handle complex information from a variety of sources?

- ◆ Can you conduct research? (find information, synthesize/analyze/evaluate, use proper documentation techniques)

- ◆ If given a visual (chart, graph, map, diagram) with a text, can you use *both* the visual *and* the text to interpret the information?

- ◆ Have you read literature from many different cultures?

- ◆ Can you adjust your reading rate, to suit the purpose?

- ◆ Can you adjust and manipulate your style of language, to suit the purpose and audience?

- ◆ Can you write reports, feature articles, etc.?

- ◆ Can you interpret and apply figurative language?

- ◆ Can you compare and contrast similar texts?

- ◆ Can you understand implications and subtext?

- ◆ Can you make assumptions and test them, given new information?

- ◆ Have you read literature from many genres? Do you know how to recognize various genres, what to expect from them, and how to distinguish among them?

- ◆ Can you discuss literature thematically (not just giving a plot summary) and can you use literary terminology in your discussion?

- ◆ Can you evaluate literature (or a speech) based upon certain criteria? Can you establish criteria for a given purpose of evaluation?

- Can you hear and appreciate the many dialects and styles of the English language?

- Can you discern and present a controlling idea in two or more similar (or seemingly dissimilar) works?

- Can you read the author/speaker's tone?

- Can you use and understand language presented in a variety or organizational patterns?

- Can you speak and write Standard English?

- Can you apply the conventions of Standard English effectively?

SUMMARY

The Standards work toward getting students to use the English language with fluency, variety, and flexibility. By *fluency*, we mean that students are able to express themselves in clear Standard English. By *variety*, we mean that students are able to understand and produce the English language in more than one voice. And by *flexibility*, we mean that students are able to adjust their language to suit the purpose and audience.

Portfolio assessment is effective in demonstrating a student's knowledge and abilities. Nothing in the Standards language implies that students have to express what they know and can do *within a specified amount of time*. The beat-the-clock nature of traditional tests limits what students can show about their abilities. But a portfolio, compiled over time, represents a fuller range of competencies and growth.

4

PORTFOLIOS

CHAPTER OVERVIEW

Many teachers who use performance tasks are interested in having students develop portfolios. This chapter describes six types of portfolios:

+ Long-term

+ Short-term

+ Compilations

+ Personal

+ Professional

+ Interdisciplinary

In addition, the chapter presents a rubric for portfolios.

A word about portfolios in the professional world: One of the reasons for the current enthusiasm about portfolios is that the very word evokes a sense of professionalism—the artist's portfolio, the architect's portfolio, and, of course, the investor's portfolio. We need to remember that all of these formalized collections that we know as portfolios, are contextual and fluid—their contents change, depending upon the purpose.

The power of portfolio assessment lies in the student's commitment to its content and appearance. Otherwise, what we call a *portfolio* might just as well be called a *folder*. A portfolio represents a *purposeful* collection, containing artifacts of student learning. The student arranges and comments upon these artifacts and presents them in an attractive way that invites readers in. The portfolio bespeaks a revisiting of past works and a metacognitive awareness of growth. Lest the portfolio degrade into a folder of stuffed papers, we need to keep in mind that the student has to care about its presentation in an ongoing way.

THE LONG-TERM PORTFOLIO

When we speak of the long-term portfolio, we are usually referring to a collection of work over the entire year, or even over more than one year. As the year progresses, the students keep their work, graded versions as well as some drafts, and they periodically review, revise, and reflect.

At the end of the year the student presents the collection of organized representative samples of work. Viewed as a whole, this volume answers the `question: *What have you learned in English this year?* The portfolio is not necessarily a collection of greatest hits, although it can be that. But it can display the worst as well as the best. We assess the long-term portfolio on presentation, completeness, progress, and reflection (see the rubric at the end of this chapter).

We don't limit the long-term portfolio to formal written work. It can contain videotapes, audiotapes, photographs, sketches, charts and graphs. It can have informal notes, reader response, even photocopies of passages out of novels that the student feels were particularly important in answering the question: *What have I learned in English this year?*

You've already graded the pieces in the long-term portfolio, so you won't be reading them with red pen in hand again, if that's what worries you (and it worried me, when I first saw these collections piled up). What you will be seeing for the first time are the table of contents and reflective pieces.

The reflective pieces serve as a guide to the portfolio. The student inserts annotated comments, transitioning from one piece to the next. Tab these comments or write them on different-colored paper, so that they are easy to find as you peruse the volume. The pages can be bound in a three-ring binder, or even placed inside a decorated box. I've heard of teachers who use empty pizza boxes for portfolios, but you'd need a lot of space for those.

The long-term portfolio is an enormously rich and satisfying project that has limitless opportunities for imaginative interpretation. The presentation of the long-term portfolio should be as formal as possible and should have students reading and commenting on each other's work. Students can assist each other in portfolio organization, and then write forwards for their buddies.

As with any complicated paperwork system, it's best to keep it simple in the beginning and limit the contents to not more than five items or so, plus the reflective pieces. You may choose to use portfolios in place of final exam, or as a portion of a final exam grade.

THE SHORT-TERM PORTFOLIO

A short-term portfolio collects materials over a period of anywhere from a couple of weeks to a month or so. There are two types of short-term portfolios: thematic and multiple revision.

A thematic portfolio could be series of tasks on a particular book, subject, or idea:

♦ A collection of character sketches of a particular novel.

♦ A series of internal monologues voiced by one character, showing that character's inner conflicts and resolutions at various points in the novel.

♦ A collection of performance tasks on a particular theme, such as *darkness*, that represents a specified number of works of literature from the same, or different, genre(s).

♦ A collection of reviews of books in a particular subgenre.

♦ A mini-anthology of original pieces with a common theme.

♦ An autobiography or biography consisting of several written artifacts (see the section on personal portfolios).

♦ A collection of various types of performance tasks related to a particular author or from a single volume, such as *The New Yorker* magazine or a newspaper.

A multiple revision portfolio consists of a baseline (first draft) followed by several purposeful revisions. The student isn't just rewriting several times, hoping that something good will happen eventually. One pattern for guided revision on a descriptive piece is:

♦ Revise to create a unified mood: Each sentence should have at least one image that is directly related to a particular mood; *then*

♦ Revise for more interesting vocabulary: Establish the proper balance among the three kinds of word types in the English language: Anglo/Saxon (used predominantly), Latinate and Greek (used in moderation); *then*

♦ Revise for figurative language: Incorporate imagery, irony, euphony, contrast; *then*

♦ Revise for sentence structure variety: Begin sentences with various grammatical structures, use a variety of punctuation, vary sentence lengths.

Another approach to multiple revision is to revise three times: first for *simplicity*, second for *clarity*, and third for *intensity*. To simplify, we get rid of superfluous words, especially modifiers. To clarify, we use nouns and verbs that are more precise. And to intensify, we use contrasting images. The *simplify, clarify, intensify* sequence works well with descriptive writing.

COMPILATION PORTFOLIO

The compilation is a student-edited anthology of published writing, photography, or music. The student selects a theme. It could be something physical, such as flowers; or historical, such as The Great Depression; or philosophical, such as honor; or emotional, such as fear. The compilation may include commentary and captions. This type of portfolio doesn't have to be in book form; it could be a display.

One good idea is to have the theme be something that arises from a major work of literature. For example, *To Kill a Mockingbird* suggests all of the above examples. It then becomes a *related readings* volume that future classes can use. Since the compilation is not personal in nature, many students might not mind leaving it behind for your future students to read as an introduction to the novel.

PERSONAL PORTFOLIO

A personal portfolio doesn't have to be written entirely by the subject: a student can ask family members, friends, and teachers to contribute memories and artifacts to such a collection. It can consist of a combination of original, as well as published, materials. These artifacts, such as ticket stubs and greeting cards, can inspire ideas for writing.

A personal portfolio can take the form of an annotated photo album or scrapbook, forming a personal yearbook, which can be long- or short-term. One effective way to manage the personal portfolio is to work on it for one week each quarter.

The obvious advantage of the personal portfolio is that the students usually have a high degree of motivation, because the subject is themselves and their own world and language. The pedagogical challenge is to extend the content and expression beyond previous knowledge. Part of the reflective piece should address what the student learned from new sources, sources outside his own known cultural universe.

PROFESSIONAL PORTFOLIO

Students who want to find after school or summer employment might wish to put together a resume along with letters of recommendation in a professional portfolio. This type of project is an opportunity to teach students to write in a crisp, businesslike style and to demonstrate care in presentation. The professional portfolio should include a short autobiographical statement and/or statement of goals. The purpose of this is to demonstrate writing proficiency. Some jobs that are popular with teenagers, such as lifeguarding, may seem not to require writing. But lifeguards do have to occasionally file incident reports, and any prospective employer is impressed by a teenager's display of clear thinking and attention to detail.

The professional portfolio is also an opportunity for the student to learn how to request, and express gratitude for, a letter of recommendation.

INTERDISCIPLINARY PORTFOLIO

As English teachers, we shouldn't miss opportunities to recognize, collect, and review writing in the content areas. An interdisciplinary portfolio can be a *greatest hits* collection from several subject areas, or it can represent a specific interdisciplinary project.

Entries could include exemplars of lab reports, complicated math problems with narrative, document-based social studies essays, writings in a language other than English, or music and art reviews. At least one of these *imports* could be required for the long-term portfolio.

The specs of the portfolio, whatever type it is, will fall into categories that can be assessed with a rubric.

A RUBRIC FOR PORTFOLIOS

- ◆ Content: The portfolio consists of the required quantity and types of material.

    4. _____

    3. _____

    2. _____

    1. _____

- ◆ Organization: The items are presented in a logical and orderly sequence, with the components clearly labeled.

    4. _____

    3. _____

    2. _____

    1. _____

♦ Presentation: The portfolio is neat and attractive, representing care and pride in presentation.

4. _____

3. _____

2. _____

1. _____

♦ Reflection: The reflective pieces show insight into your learning style, progress, and areas in need if improvement.

4. _____

3. _____

2. _____

1. _____

SUMMARY

Performance tasks can be made more meaningful if they are purposefully and formally assembled into a portfolio. As in the professional world, portfolios serve various purposes and are of various types. By compiling portfolios, students take performance tasks one step further. A novice teacher need not feel overwhelmed by the thought of portfolio assessment. She can start off small, with any number of short-term alternatives.

Once our assessments include portfolios, we can integrate interdisciplinary learning and multiple intelligence theory into curriculum design.

5

MULTIPLE INTELLIGENCE APPROACHES

CHAPTER OVERVIEW

Performance tasks in English language arts offer the perfect opportunity for tapping into multiple intelligence approaches. These modes of intelligence are interconnected, and educational theorists are considering adding other types of intelligence to the list.

1. Verbal-Linguistic

   This is intelligence that comes through words. Obviously, English Language Arts tasks are almost always centered on this type of knowing. Traditional tasks are essays, debates, speeches, dramatics, creative writing. Humor based on satire and wordplay is also part of verbal-linguistic intelligence.

2. Intrapersonal

   This is the knowing of the self. Reflective pieces that call for meta-cognition (thinking about thinking) tap into this kind of intelligence, as do autobiographical pieces. Philosophical and spiritual thinking is also in this realm. Tasks that call for knowing of the self are journals, especially reader response journals, which ask the student to justify an opinion, react on an emotional level, or relate the self to the literature.

3. Interpersonal

   This is intelligence that involves communicating with and having insight into others. Students with this strength do well in cooperative learning groups; they make good leaders, but they also make good group members. Tasks that ask the student to perceive the nature of relationships among characters, to understand conflict, and to analyze character traits focus on interpersonal intelligence.

4. Musical-Rhythmic

    This is knowing the world through sound and rhythm. Any good piece of writing, not just poetry, has rhythm. Every sentence has an intonational contour, and the careful writer knows where to place the words of emphasis. Those with this strength can see patterns of sound and can find the relationship between music and meaning. Asking students to soundtrack a story is a powerful way of leading them to find various interpretations. Language is filled with metaphors of sound and music. These metaphors abound in advertising, poetry, editorial writing, and reviews.

5. Bodily-Kinesthetic

    This is knowing through physicality and performance. In English class, the handiest form of this type of intelligence is dramatics. Students usually enjoy making videos or acting out live presentations of the literature. People with a strong bodily-kinesthetic way of understanding the world concretize an intellectual concept, such as a new vocabulary word, by acting it out.

6. Visual-Spatial

    This is knowing the world through mental and actual pictures. We often hear people refer to themselves as *visual learners*. Such learning involves making and responding to illustrations, flow charts, symbols, and other graphic representations. We should remind students to activate the *movie of the mind* and to use vivid imagery, even if the writing piece is not designated as descriptive.

7. Logical-Mathematical

    This is knowing the world through patterns and numbers. A *number person* can express the complexities of literature and language through intricate diagrams and tessellations. She can also understand that effective sentence making is a matter of expressing relationships between subordinate and main ideas. Many syntactical concepts, such as parallel structure, have a logical-mathematical base.

8. Naturalistic

This is knowing the world through nature. A strong naturalistic learner can perceive patterns and subtleties in the outdoor world. She can make predictions, gather evidence, and draw conclusions based on the complex relationships in nature. She has a keen sense of orientation and sharp observational skills.

Although I've listed eight discrete types of intelligence, the door is open to others, such as knowing the world through aesthetics. Multiple intelligence pedagogy is an emergent field.

IMPLICATIONS

Although our subject is implicitly verbal/linguistic, many, if not all, of the other ways of knowing can come into play and make our students stronger learners. You may wish to consider the following implications of multiple intelligence theory as you plan performance tasks:

- Metacognition

  Students become stronger learners when they understand their own learning styles. A student who has trouble concentrating on reading a novel may do well by charting the action on a graphic organizer, but she may not be aware that such a method would help her understand the story. As you offer students choices and as you combine traditional verbal/linguistic tasks with those that reach into the other intelligences, ask students to reflect on how they learned.

- Student Choices

  As a closing activity for a major literary unit, such as a novel or Shakespearean play, you may wish to offer many choices for performance tasks which embrace multiple intelligences. Figure 5.1 (pp. 58–59) is a list of supplemental projects for *The Hobbit* and other journey stories and Figure 5.2 (pp. 60–62) is a list of supplemental projects for the *Hunchback of Notre Dame*.

(Text continues on page 62.)

FIGURE 5.1. SUPPLEMENTAL PROJECTS: *THE HOBBIT* AND OTHER JOURNEY STORIES

1. PowerPoint Presentation (*Verbal/linguistic; visual/spatial*)

   You may do a PowerPoint presentation on any aspect of the journey story genre. Show that you understand the hallmarks of the genre. Have at least 12 slides.

2. Flowchart (*Verbal/linguistic; visual/spatial; logical/mathematical*)

   Express the ideas of *The Hobbit* in the form of a flow chart or other graphic representation. You may choose all or parts of the book. Be sure to show how various events, characters, and settings are related.

3. Venn Diagram (Comparison Contrast) (*Verbal/linguistic; visual/spatial*)

   The novel centers around the real world and the world of the journey. In two overlapping circles, list the commonalties and differences in the aspects of both worlds.

4. Bulletin Board Display (*Verbal/linguistic; visual/spatial*)

   Make a bulletin board display that expresses one of the following: a unified theme of the novel; the cast of characters; the setting; the major events. Be sure that the title is clear. The display should make the book look as interesting as possible, inviting others to read it.

5. Video (*Verbal/linguistic; bodily/kinesthetic; interpersonal*)

   Enact a scene or coming attractions (3 to 5 minutes).

6. Creative Writing/Found Language (*Verbal/linguistic; musical/rhythmic*)

   Using specific, interesting words and phrases found in the literature, compose a poem, description, or story. Be sure that your piece is *inspired* by the literature, but not *about* the literature. Italicize the language taken from the literature.

7. Journalizing a Fictitious Character (*Verbal/linguistic; interpersonal*)

   Select a specific character at a specific time (or at various times) and write journal entries that indicate how that character experiences the events which the character is in the midst of. Be sure to focus on interesting turning points of the character. (Don't pick a mundane day in the life of the character.)

8. Journalism (*Verbal/linguistic; visual/spatial*)

   Make a front page for any point in the story. You may use Word 6.0 Newsletter Wizard for layout.

9. Dramatic Presentation (*Verbal/linguistic; bodily/kinesthetic; interpersonal*)

   Present a scene for the class (3 to 5 minutes). Be sure to use props, costume pieces, and so on.

10. Literature and Self (*Verbal/linguistic/intrapersonal*)

    Explain how one of the following quotations from the story applies to the character of Bilbo Baggins as well as to yourself and your own experiences:

    - There is always more about you than anyone expects! You are not the little hobbit that you were

    - Escaping goblins to be caught by wolves!

11. Nature Trail (*Verbal/linguistic; naturalistic*)

    Make a map, chart, or guide that shows the relationship between various features of nature and the events in the story. Show that you understand how such features as mountains, valleys, caves, streams, and so forth affect what happens to the characters.

FIGURE 5.2. SUPPLEMENTAL PROJECTS: THE HUNCHBACK OF NOTRE DAME

1. Make a Glossary of Terms (*Verbal/linguistic*)

   All glossaries must have 15 terms. Each term must include the following:

   - Context: Cite the page and copy out the sentence in which the term appears.
   - Definition: When presenting the definition, be sure not to just copy out the first definition given in the dictionary. Be sure that the definition is appropriate to the context.
   - Illustration: If applicable
   - Significance: Explain how this term is relevant to the story. How does this term/concept fit into the ideas or events of the story?

   If you choose to do a glossary, you may choose any *one* of the following categories:

   - Architecture
   - Mythology
   - Terms of the Church

2. Comparison/Contrast (*Verbal/linguistic; visual/spatial*)

   Draw two large circles which overlap approximately ⅓ of their areas. In the non-overlapping areas of each circle, list elements of the stories below which are not shared in common (differences). In the overlapping areas, list elements of the stories which are shared in common. Be as specific as possible. You may compare/contrast the following stories to *Hunchback:*

   - *Beauty and the Beast*
   - *Phantom of the Opera*
   - *Les Miserables*

3. The Disney *Hunchback:*

   You may write a report of approx. 2 pages in which you deal with the following aspects of the Disney movie:

   - Discuss the differences between the film and the book. Explain the changes that were made and speculate on why you think those changes were made. Give a brief critique of the film.

- Compare the Disney *Hunchback of Notre Dame* with at least two other Disney films.

- Consider visual impact, the story, the characters, the music, and so on. (*Visual/spatial; rhythmic/musical*)

- Consider the lyrics of the songs. How do they establish the meaning of the story in terms of theme, character development, and overall affect? Include lyrics of at least one song (*Rhythmic/musical*)

- Consider the visual qualities of the film. How does the animation capture the pictures described by Victor Hugo? Refer to specific passages and compare them to specific scenes. (*Visual/spatial*)

4. Translate several paragraphs into French (*Verbal/linguistic*)

5. Creative Writing (*Verbal/linguistic; intrapersonal*)

   Find several (approximately 10) phrases or words from the story that intrigue you and list them. Let these phrases marinate for one day. Then, looking at your list with fresh eyes, compose a poem or story that incorporates these words. The piece that you write should *not* be about *Hunchback*.

6. Video (*Verbal/linguistic; bodily/kinesthetic; interpersonal*)

   Produce a five-minute video that consists of either a specific scene, or coming attractions.

7. Bulletin Board Display (*Visual/spatial*)

   Make an attractive and readable classroom poster that illustrates some aspect of *Hunchback*. Include key words from the story. For example, illustrate one particularly interesting sentence from the book.

8. Journalism (*Visual/spatial; verbal/linguistic*)

   Write a front-page account of the climactic scene that ends the novel. Include headlines, captions, and pictures.

9. Journalizing (*Verbal/linguistic; interpersonal*)

   Write three detailed journal entries for either three different characters or for one character at three different points in the story. Use authentic language. You may choose to recount the same event from three different character's eyes.

10. PowerPoint Presentation (*Verbal/linguistic; visual/spatial*)

   Make a slide (PowerPoint) presentation on a particular aspect of the book or its background. Have at least 10 slides.

11. Flowchart (*Verbal/linguistic; visual/spatial*)

   Express the events of all or part of the story in the form of a flowchart which clearly communicates the sequence of events.

12. Nature Metaphors (*Verbal/linguistic; naturalistic*)

   Identify at least 10 metaphors that refer to nature. For each, explain the implications of the metaphor and its power: What does each represent and why is the metaphor apt?

THE CLASSROOM COMMUNITY

Because many of the multiple intelligences involve communication, it is essential that there be a positive classroom tone. This is a subtle area of good classroom management, which teachers can foster in various ways. The physical set-up of the room is much more conducive to communication if desks are arranged in clusters or a horseshoe so that students can see each other's faces, rather than just the backs of heads. Teachers who admit mistakes, have a sense of humor about themselves, and don't give the impression that they know everything, are likely to evoke a spirit of collegiality in their students. This positive atmosphere encourages questions, observations, and connections. Multiple intelligence awareness is community building because it shows respect for student strengths and individuality.

The English classroom is the perfect place for community building. Think about it. Where else does a group of people assemble in order to discuss their reactions to and interpretations of a work of literature that all of them (well, *most*...OK, *some*) have read (...part of)?

As you go through the performance tasks in the next section, consider how students can work cooperatively on the projects themselves, where applicable, or how they can share or display what they've completed.

SUMMARY

Multiple intelligence theory is an important component of curriculum design in a performance-based classroom. It respects the student's strengths, interests, and individuality. By giving students choices, we generate various projects, and each of these projects, as it is presented to the class as a whole, becomes another way to reinforce learning.

PART II

A COLLECTION OF PERFORMANCE TASKS AND RUBRICS

This section presents detailed performance tasks, directions to the students, guides for instruction, scoring guides (rubrics) and other helpful comments that will assist your planning and help establish expectations for you and your students. The tasks are divided into these following categories:

- ♦ Performance tasks based on....
  - Journalism
  - Poetry
  - Syntax
  - Literary Criticism
  - Shakespeare

You will also find samples of student work at various levels of proficiency as well as teacher comments and suggestions for remediation. The suggestions for remediation show how you can scaffold the learning to meet the needs of students who are having difficulty, while maintaining the intellectual integrity of the task.

6

PERFORMANCE TASKS BASED ON JOURNALISM

CHAPTER OVERVIEW

A good newspaper is a gold mine for performance tasks, representing, as it does, many genres and subgenres of nonfiction writing. Sorting out these genres and being able to identify their features is a performance task in itself. This chapter presents four performance tasks based on journalism:

- The investigative report: research and planning

- Writing a film review

ABOUT INVESTIGATIVE REPORTS

Investigative reports are a specialized form of journalism because, unlike breaking news stories, investigative reports represent research gathered and sifted over a period of time. Investigative reports tend to be long (approximately 1,000 words), may be serialized, and are less time-sensitive than breaking news stories.

Matthew Wald's "Setting Limits on Teen-Age Drivers" (*New York Times*, June 5, 1998) is a feature article that explains controversies and policies regarding licensing of teenaged drivers. Many states, in response to alarming accident rates among teenage drivers, have instituted a system called graduated licensing. This means that the probationary (or restricted) period would be extended and that the young driver might have to prove himself more stringently over time. Some states require more than one road test; others place limits on the number and age of passengers that teenagers at the wheel are permitted to have.

If we scour the newspaper daily for performance task opportunities, we can find articles such as Matthew Wald's article. Few topics are more motivating to high school students than driver eligibility. Here is a synopsis of the article and performance tasks that grow out of it.

65

SYNOPSIS

"Congress and the state legislatures have bogged down in their efforts to pass new laws on a risky group of drivers, those who drive drunk. But lawmakers are still voting new restrictions on another group who have a disproportionate share of auto accidents: teenagers."

With this as the opening paragraph, Wald cites some anecdotal reports by people who have been victimized by inept teenage drivers. He gives statistics from the American Automobile Association on the high rate of fatal crashes that involve teenagers at the wheel. Focusing on the state of Wisconsin, Wald makes comparisons between teen-age driving mishaps and those involving DWI; he also compares the number hours required to receive a haircutting license (1,000) to the mere 6 hours that the state of Wisconsin requires for earning a driver's license.

An investigative report is the result of interviews. Wald develops his report with personal anecdotes as well as the testimony of professionals in the field of transportation safety. Thus, he balances emotionally charged material with statistics and legal language. He refers to specific studies and cites various laws and campaigns to change them.

Wald ends with a quotation by Mark Edwards, AAA's managing director for traffic safety:"We really know you learn how to drive by driving, not by reading books about it," Mr. Edwards said. What beginners need most, is "more time behind the wheel."

RESEARCHING AND PLANNING THE INVESTIGATIVE REPORT

PRODUCT: TO DO LIST OF THE INVESTIGATIVE REPORTER

In this task, students analyze the investigative report entitled "Setting Limits on Teen-Age Drivers" by Matthew Wald (*New York Times,* June 5, 1998) and make a list of what the journalist had to do to complete the research on this project.

DIRECTIONS TO THE STUDENT

Pretend that you are Matthew Wald, the journalist who wrote "Setting Limits on Teen-Age Drivers." It is the beginning of the project: your proposal has been accepted. Now, it's time for you to make a *to do* list for yourself. Make a bulleted list of tasks that the investigative reporter had to do before he could start writing.

INSTRUCTION

This task calls for a thorough analysis of the report. Each paragraph contains information that the reporter had to find somewhere. To instruct for this task, you will need to point out the various sources of information, and how to reach credentialed people. The key questions are: *What do we need to know?* and *Where can we find it?*

STANDARDS

This task addresses the standards because it requires research and critical reading skills. It requires the reader to sort out the roles of the various people mentioned in the article. This task is what the pre-writing stage of the writing process looks like for the investigative reporter.

CHALLENGES

This task is accessible to students who do not have strong reading and writing skills. The student has to ask, after each paragraph: "What did the journalist have to do to find this out?" This is a good task for students who need to begin thinking on an inferential level.

MULTIPLE INTELLIGENCES

The reading comprehension component of this task involves verbal-linguistic intelligence. Students who are strong in logical-mathematical intelligence might want to use a chart or graph to figure out what they need to know and where to find it. Most investigative reports do accompany text with a visual showing mathematical information.

SCORING GUIDES

- ◆ Meaning and Development: You've provided sufficient information that would be needed to run an investigative report.

    4. _____

    3. _____

    2. _____

    1. _____

- ◆ Organization: You've presented the steps to the investigative report in a logical order; you've used parallel structure.

    4. _____

    3. _____

    2. _____

    1. _____

- ◆ Word Choice: You've used the terminology that is used in the article.

    4. _____

    3. _____

    2. _____

    1. _____

- ◆ Presentation: Your list is set up so that it is easy to follow.

    4. _____

    3. _____

    2. _____

    1. _____

FOLLOW-UP

To make this pre-writing activity more detailed, students can make a questionnaire and/or write telephone interview questions. They can also make a checklist with room for notes and an outline. Because investigative reporting is sometimes a collaborative effort, students can work in pairs and develop a division of labor plan. They won't actually be carrying out this plan, as this particular report has already been done, but they can apply their plan to a real report on a topic of their choosing. Even if the task ends with the division of labor plan, they will have considered how much work goes into each stage of the research process.

SAMPLES OF STUDENT WORK

JUSTIN: HIGH LEVEL

- For regulations, current laws and provisions: Make a list of authorities and find out names of PR people:
  - A.A.A.
  - National Transportation Safety Board
  - Car Insurance companies
  - Motor Vehicle Bureaus
- For anecdotal reports: locate affected parties: teenagers and their parents, victims of accidents involving teen-age drivers
- Get facts: statistics, dates, place names, surveys
- Get examples of regulations from various states
- Compare teen-age drivers and other high risk groups, such as drunk drivers
- Compare learning to drive and learning other complicated skills

COMMENTARY

Justin's list is well organized, concise, logical, and easy to follow. Particularly strong is his emphasis on verbs, showing what needs to be done. Justin has done an excellent job of analyzing the investigative report and gleaning from it the exact tasks that the reporter had to do. He shows a close reading of the report by naming specific agencies. An impressive touch is the distinguishing between the authorities and the ordinary citizens affected by the issue of inept drivers.

KARA: MID LEVEL

- Find out who to call to get info
  - A.A.A.
  - Car Insurance companies
  - Motor Vehicle Bureaus
  - People who have had accidents involving young drivers
- Get all statistics
- Find out about state regs

COMMENTARY

Kara far less detailed than was Justin, but she has a fairly good sense of what has to be done. She leaves off the National Transportation Safety Board, which is a key agency, and she omits the sections of the report that involve comparisons between groups of drivers and between learning to drive and learning other skills.

CERESE: LOW LEVEL

For my report I have to get information. I had to find out how many teenagers had accidents and why. I have to look up laws. How do teenagers get there lisence? Is it the same for every state? Many people think that there should be different laws for teenagers. That teenagers should take longer to get there lisence. In this report I am going to talk about why people are mad that teenagers get in so many accidence.

COMMENTARY

Cerese's mechanical errors may show a gap in her learning that has to be addressed. By making a paragraph, she signals that she doesn't really understand the purpose of the task or the audience (herself). This is far too general to serve its intended purpose, and does not show a grounding in the text.

REMEDIATION

What might help Cerese here is to point out that although we *usually* want complete sentences, this time we're better off without them. Using a paragraph structure, students might lapse into narrative at the expense of necessary detail. We might want to head up a bulleted list with the words *find out...people to contact*. Also, we need to clarify that one of the purposes of this task is to show close reading of the article. Kara should be able to check off specific information that she couldn't have known without comprehending the text. She can use a hi-liter to indicate this information on her to-do lists.

WRITING A FILM REVIEW

PRODUCT: FILM REVIEW

In this task, students write a five-paragraph film review

DIRECTIONS TO THE STUDENT

In class, we will be reading several reviews of movies that are currently playing in the theaters. As we read the reviews, you will note what a reviewer communicates to the readers about the film. We will make a list of features of a film review and then you will write a review of a new movie of your choice. You are free to choose a movie about which we've already read a review.

INSTRUCTION

To complete this task, the students need to learn the features of the film review genre After reading several reviews, students will notice that most reviews display these features:

- A literary title for the review: play on words, alliteration, vivid image, etc.

- An intriguing opening that sets the stage for the film

- The director and stars; other films associated with them

- The place of this film in its genre: What other films are like it?

- A synopsis and brief descriptions of key scenes

- Audience appeal. What type of audience will like this film? What will be their expectations? Will these expectations be met, or will a particular audience be disappointed.

- The closing paragraph conveys the reviewer's overall recommendation.

Film reviews have short paragraphs, lively language with plenty of metaphor, and an enthusiastic tone.

Note the following conventions of the film review genre:

- The title of the film is set off in quotation marks.

- The review includes conventional information: Number of stars and what that number indicates, e.g., ***(good); rating; length in minutes; director, principal actors, and studio

- Sometimes, the review is broken up by headings and/or pull quotes.

- Casual language is used, permitting contractions and colloquialisms.

- The reviewer's opinion is interspersed with the summary and key scenes.

- The review is written in the third person.

An indispensable part of instruction is *analyzing the models*. Without this, students are likely to produce no more than a summary with their opinion tacked on.

REGARDING PLAGIARISM

How do we know that the student hasn't plagiarized his film review? A professional review will probably contain language that is slicker and more professional than what most high school students could produce. A professional review is usually targeted to a general audience, rather than to a high school audience.

Students sometimes grab a sentence or paragraph from a professional source, and, when they do, there is a glaring difference in style between their original voice and that of the professional. This offers the opportunity to teach (and it's best done before the fact) the conventions of parenthetical attribution.

I've said that part of good instruction is to present several model reviews. If these models are of contemporary films, perhaps your students will credit you with having access to any reviews they might want to plagiarize, an assumption which is actually true. Or, perhaps they will figure that any review they could plagiarize could also be submitted by another like-minded student.

Plagiarism is always a stubborn problem, and not likely to leave us soon, if ever. Some teachers get around the problem by requiring that all or part of easily-copied writing tasks be composed in class.

STANDARDS

This task requires students to substantiate their opinions and at the same time, consider what the opinion of their audience is likely to be on a particular film. They need to deduce the features and conventions of a film review as a genre, and then write in a style that conforms. They need to understand how a movie fits into other movies of its type: What in the film is recognizable and predictable? They need to use lively language that captures key scenes without giving away too much of the story. And they need to convey what the film has to offer on an emotional level. They need to vary vocabulary beyond *good, bad, boring, sad,* and *funny.* And they need to know something about the history of film: What else did this director direct? Is this film a remake of an earlier classic? What scenes in what other films does it evoke?

CHALLENGES

This is a highly sophisticated task. The challenge to the student is to write a review that has pithy and vivid language and that substantiates his opinion without just saying, in effect, "It was good because I liked it." The reviewer has to make sophisticated assumptions about the film's intended audience and whether that intended audience will appreciate the film. The student reviewer has to reveal his cultural literacy about the traditions of filmdom without sounding pretentious.

MULTIPLE INTELLIGENCES

Writing the review requires verbal-linguistic intelligence. Students with strong visual-spatial intelligence will be good at interpreting visual symbols, remembering details of scenes, and using language that describes visual imagery.

SCORING GUIDE

- ◆ Meaning and Development: You've provided all of the information that is expected in a film review. (Note that the information is not spelled out in the rubric. To do so would make the rubric too task specific. The idea is for the student to *know* what is expected, based on the deductive analysis of the models.)

    4. _____

    3. _____

    2. _____

    1. _____

- ◆ Audience Awareness: You show an understanding of the needs and interests of the people who would be likely to read this review.

    4. _____

    3. _____

    2. _____

    1. _____

♦ Organization: Your first and last paragraphs have the most important information. Your organizational structure is similar to that of the model reviews.

4. _____

3. _____

2. _____

1. _____

♦ Word Choice: You've used figurative language, vivid words that capture the reader's attention, and words appropriate to the world of film.

4. _____

3. _____

2. _____

1. _____

♦ Conventions: You've observed the rules of spelling, capitalization, punctuation, paragraphing and presentation. You've followed the conventions of the genre.

4. _____

3. _____

2. _____

1. _____

FOLLOW-UP

Film reviews can be oral as well as written. The Siskel and Ebert format, which has two reviewers who may or may not agree with each other, can be presented live or on videotape. Students can learn to write other kinds of reviews: on books, music, sporting events, restaurants, and travel spots.

SAMPLES OF STUDENT WORK
TAMAR: HIGH LEVEL

"Big Baby"

A Review of "Big Daddy"
Colombia Pictures
Rated PG (crude humor, language)
Starring Adam Sandler
Written by Tim Herlihy, Adam Sandler, Steve Franks
Directed by Dennis Dugan

People who go to Adam Sandler movies, well…go to Adam Sandler movies. You can expect to get your money's worth if you like the usual Sandler fare. And if you don't know what that is, then you probably won't like "Big Daddy." Once again we have Sandler playing an underachiever making a lifestyle out of avoiding adult responsibilities.

The Sandler character plays, Sonny Koufax, is a law school graduate working as a toll booth collector who decides to up his sex appeal and prove his worthiness (sound familiar?) by adopting a five-year-old orphan, whom he immediately decides to un-adopt. As you can easily predict, the kid grows on Big Daddy, probably because they are both on the same maturity level.

We have the usual suspects. What would a Sandler joint be without Steve Buscemi? Sandler trivia buffs know that Buscemi played the crazed, lipstick-smearing save-the-day gunman in "Billy Madison" as well as the drunken brother-of-the-groom in "The Wedding Singer." Here, he's the ever-present street bum and his performance is hilarious. And we have another appearance by the wild-looking Josh Mostel, whom we recognize as the school administrator in "Billy Madison."

Although many serious film critics turn their noses up at Adam Sandler, dismissing him as just another maker of teen-age gross-out films, there's a touching side to this one (and to the other ones, too). There's even a courtroom custody scene that might give you an unexpected lump in your throat.

What you expect is what you get in a Sandler film, so if you like public urination, crass humor, and a heavy dose of sentimentality, then you'll like "Big Daddy" as much as I did.

COMMENTARY

Tamar succeeds at speaking in a lively, comical voice, well suited to the tone of the film. She places the film in his context by referring to other Adam Sandler movies and the actors in them. She gives a thumbnail sketch along with a reference to a key scene. After reading this review, you'd have a good idea of what to expect from this film and who its intended audience is. Note the clever title as well as the inclusion of traditional film information.

LUCIEN: MID LEVEL

Adam Sandler is the "Big Daddy"

Adam Sandler's new movie is "Big Daddy" and it's a lot like all the other Adam Sandler movies such as "Water Boy," "Billy Madison," "The Wedding Singer," and "Happy Gilmore."

In this movie Adam Sandler plays a man named Sonny Koufax. Sandy Koufax was a famous baseball player in the 60s. Sonny is a toll collector but he graduated from law school. His girlfriend breaks up with him because he's too immature so he adopts a child. As soon as he adopts the child he realize that he doesn't want the responsibility but it's too late. He has to keep the kid.

Most of the movie was very funny but parts of it were sad. Like when they go to court for a custody battle. I won't tell you what happens. You have to see it, and if you like the other Adam Sandler movies you will like this one.

COMMENTARY

Lucien's review does not display the facility with language that Tamar had, but he does show an understanding of who the audience is and what to expect. He doesn't have the requisite five paragraphs, and omits the details of the secondary characters in the film. Note the omission of traditional film information preceding the review.

NELL: LOW LEVEL

"Big Daddy"

"Big Daddy" staring Adam Sandler is about a man who adopts a child and wants to give him back. But when you adopt a child you can't give him back it's just not that easy. In this movie Adam Sandler wants to impress his girlfriend so he adopts a kid. The kid is played by twins one at a time. They do that in movies because one kid might get cranky so they have another identical one to take his place.

I thought the movie was stupid but funny. I like the part where he's yelling at the kid.

COMMENTARY

There's not much reason to believe that Nell saw the film. She makes no attempt at placing the film in any context or in adhering to the format of the genre. Note the omission of traditional information as well as the lack of an original title for the review. Note also the reliance on the first person point of view.

REMEDIATION

Familiarity with other film reviews is key to writing one. Students may need a format sheet or checklist that will spell out the features of the genre. You could instruct through deductive reasoning: Have students read a *simple* review and tell what questions the review answers. For students needing remediation, it's better to work from a review from a local newspaper, which might be less sophisticated than one from the *New York Times*.

SUMMARY

Journalism in its various forms is tailor-made for performance tasks that call for higher-level thinking and meet the Standards. Some of the liveliest and most sensuous writing available is found in the sports, travel, science and food sections. Local newspapers often feature editorials, reviews, and small features written by students. Letters to the editor are more likely to be printed in local, rather than large metropolitan papers. You can compare and contrast one newspaper to another, a newspaper to a news magazine, written news to television news. Photojournalism offers high-level performance-task possibilities: What are the implications of various images in terms of placement, facial expressions, dress, and other details? Consider captions and headlines. It isn't unrealistic to expect high school students in upper-level classes to be regular readers of syndicated columnists such as William Safire or Maureen Dowd. Finally, use the newspaper instead of, or at least as a supplement to, the grammar and vocabulary workbook.

7

PERFORMANCE TASKS BASED ON POETRY

CHAPTER OVERVIEW

Whatever we learn about poetry can improve our use of every other type of language, including areas not normally associated with poetry, such as technical writing. Learning about poetry teaches us how to write and speak with rhythm, grace, subtlety, economy, wit, and heart. These are qualities that make our writing easier to comprehend and memorable.

The performance tasks presented here are designed to invite students into a poem, to make them feel welcome. When a poem's meaning is clear to us, we say it is *accessible*. If a poem is *inaccessible*, if we can't crack it open, if it disinvites us, then it is useless. These tasks are designed to get students to find their ways into the poem, to see that it is not as inaccessible as it may appear at first.

The first tenet of poetry is that a poem must be read more than once. The second tenet: read the poem aloud. The ear and the tongue give meaning that the eye alone does not see.

The third tenet of poetry is that the poem does have a meaning grounded in text, but that meaning can change, depending upon what we bring from our own experience. We are allowed to be reminded of whatever we are reminded of in the poem, but that doesn't mean that the poem itself has no objective meaning.

Reading a poem is like visiting a place for the first time. The more you visit that place, the more details you notice, the more comfortable you feel, the freer you are to explore.

The tasks in this section can be used for any poem. The tasks are:

♦ Writing a poetry explication

♦ Interview with a poem

♦ From poem to prose

♦ A Shakespearean word inventory

79

This section closes with a "poetry unwrapper," which is a set of generic questions to help students approach a poem with literary terms and traditions in mind.

WRITING A POETRY EXPLICATION

PRODUCT: LITERARY ESSAY

In this task, students will select one of several poems by the same poet or on the same theme. They will write a literary essay of four to five paragraphs that explicates the meaning of the poem and uses literary terms.

DIRECTIONS TO THE STUDENTS

Write a literary essay of four or five paragraphs that explains the meaning of the poem you have selected. In your essay, express your understanding of the poem's controlling idea. Refer to literary elements such as theme, characterization, structure, point of view and techniques such as symbolism, irony, figurative language. Explain how these elements and techniques convey the controlling idea. Discuss both obvious and subtle meanings of the poem as well your personal response to it. In discussing your personal response, don't just say that you liked or didn't like the poem; tell how the poem relates to your own experience and why.

INSTRUCTION

Etymologically, the word *explicate* means to *fold (plic) out (ex)*, which is exactly what we are doing here. Using our literary terms as tools, we are dissecting and analyzing what the poem means objectively and what it means to us personally. We are explaining not only the obvious controlling idea but also the ambiguities of the poem.

The following is a 12-step procedure for leading students to find meaning in poetry:

1. Multiple readings

   Give the class some time to read the poem silently. Then, ask several different readers to read it aloud. As the instruction continues, you might want to hear the poem again. Multiple exposure is an important part of the poetry experience.

2. Consider the title

    Ask the class to list what they think of when they hear the title. What expectations does it set up? Are these expectations met? Does the title have a double meaning?

3. Getting in

    What is obvious about the poem? What are the ideas, images, and lines that students clearly understand? List everything that the students already know about the poem. The obvious will open the door to the subtle.

4. Questions

    Now we can consider what remains unknown. Define unfamiliar words. Consider words and phrases whose meanings are puzzling in this context. At this point, you don't have to *have answers*; sometimes, just raising the questions brings us to a more personal understanding than having the teacher *give answers*.

5. Key verbs

    Without using the phrase *is about* express the controlling idea of this poem. We avoid *is about* because the search for meaning often ends there. "This poem is about bats." Then what? A better approach is to use key poetry-talking verbs, as described below:

    -   Evoke

        The word *evoke* is an essential tool for poetry-talking. Meaning *to bring out*, we use *evoke* to explain what the poem brings out in us, what it makes us think about, or reminds us of. Students usually need some guided practice in using this word, but it's time well spent, because *evoke* elevates thinking and invites us to think about our relationship to the poem: "The images in the second stanza evoke homesickness for the ordinary family rituals that the poet misses."

    -   Convey

        When we say what a poem or image *conveys*, we make a direct hit: "The poem conveys the poet's yearning to play baseball."

    -   Suggest

        This verb gets us right into such poetic concepts as connotation, multiple meaning, and atmosphere: "The words 'quick eyes' suggest that the deer is fearful and watchful, ready to bolt."

- Portray

  To use *portray* is to show that we understand the pictures evoked by the words: "The poem portrays life in a small town."

6. The *I think of…* statement

    The reader will develop a stronger sense of meaning if given the opportunity to let the poem into his own world. This is where the *I think of…* statement comes in. Once or twice in the essay, the student should say what a particular image or idea reminds him of in his own life: "*I think of…* my first day at my new school, when I didn't know anyone and I was afraid to open my mouth."

7. Use of literary terms

    By this time, students are deep into the meaning of the poem and are ready to think about how its figurative language operates. They've learned to distinguish a metaphor from a simile, how to recognize personification, what alliteration and onomatopoeia are, but now they need to show how these techniques actually work in a real poem. This means thinking about *effects:* "The poet refers to 'the loss of the moon to the dark hands of Chicago.' This personification evokes darkness, industrialization, detachment, aloneness." If the poem has an allusion, then the source of the allusion bears a meaning that enriches the poem: "The title 'Rachel of the Sea' evokes the end of *Moby Dick,* when the ship the *Rachel* rescues the floundering Ishmael."

8. Use of conventions

    Now would be the time to show students how to quote from a poem and use proper punctuation and capitalization to do so. Because they have to justify their statements with text, they should have three or four such quotations in their explication.

9. Contrast

    Almost all poems have contrast. Contrasts can appear in such poetic devices as irony, juxtaposition, and oxymoron. More subtle contrasts lie in the very sounds of the words themselves: harsh and soft sounds, clipped and long sounds.

10. Single word analysis

    To find out what makes a particular part of a poem tick, we can simply ask ourselves why the poet chose one specific word over another. Does it have a certain connotation? Does it alliterate, rhyme, or half rhyme? Does it work with the rhythm?

11. Literary context

The poem might be similar to, or even based on, other poems. When we ask students to find similarities between this and another poem, we reinforce their understanding of the new poem, and we also place it in a literary context. A high level class can recognize literary philosophies such as romanticism, naturalism, modernism, and so on.

12. Details

Finally, consider the details by looking at how specific the nouns of the poem are. How do these details bring the poem to life?

By now the students should have plenty of pre-writing notes and ideas from which to build their explication. They have to decide which are the most salient points for a given poem.

STANDARDS

This task meets the Standards because it involves close analysis of language qua language: how words work together to create multiple meanings, economy of words, the interplay between sound and sense. By explicating the poem, we are doing more than just summarizing it: we are engaging in higher level thinking as we hold the words up to the light of our own experience and see how they change as we handle them.

CHALLENGE LEVEL

The challenge level of a poetry explication would vary with the level of language of the poem and the student's prior knowledge. An *easy* poem might be deceptively challenging to explicate because the reader might not find much beyond its literal meaning. In any case, poetry explication is to the English class what calculus is to the math class: the ultimate challenge that takes in all of the other skills. It tests organization of an essay, intensive critical reading comprehension, use of esoteric terminology, and use of sophisticated conventions.

MULTIPLE INTELLIGENCE

Explicating a poem requires verbal-linguistic intelligence of course, but it also draws upon musical-rhythmic intelligence, as the students have to consider how rhythm contributes to meaning. Students can use bodily-kinesthetic intelligence to understand the physical sensations evoked by some poems.

SCORING GUIDE

- ◆ Meaning: You've explained the meaning of the poem by referring to literary elements and techniques.

    4. _____

    3. _____

    2. _____

    1. _____

- ◆ Development: You've discussed various aspects of the poem and provided specific references and quotations from it.

    4. _____

    3. _____

    2. _____

    1. _____

- ◆ Organization: You've organized your ideas into logical paragraph form with transitions. You have an introduction and conclusion.

    4. _____

    3. _____

    2. _____

    1. _____

- ◆ Word Choice: You've used words that are appropriate to a discussion of poetry.

    4. _____

    3. _____

    2. _____

    1. _____

- ◆ Conventions: You've followed the rules for spelling, capitalization, punctuation, and presentation.

    4. _____

    3. _____

    2. _____

    1. _____

FOLLOW-UP

In addition to following up with poetry at more sophisticated levels, the skills learned in doing a poetry explication are applicable to all literary analyses. Once students understand what goes into a poem, their own writing of poetry and prose should incorporate the techniques of figurative language.

INTERVIEW WITH A POEM

PRODUCT: A SCRIPTED INTERVIEW

In this task, two students will perform a scripted interview that explicates the meaning of a poem. One student, playing the interviewer, will ask the questions of the other, who will play the part of the poem, speaking in the first person.

DIRECTIONS TO THE STUDENTS

Working with your partner, select a poem that you think has an interesting meaning and many secrets and mysteries. Script a 10-question interview in which one of you plays the interviewer and the other speaks from the voice of the poem. That is, the person playing the part of the poem answers the questions as if the poem itself were speaking. You will perform your interview for the class. In your performance, you may *refer* to notes on index cards, but you may not *read* from the cards. Make eye contact, improvise from your notes, respond to the other person. You will have time in class to rehearse your interview. Practice proper speech; weed out *like's* and *y'know's* and other bad habits.

INSTRUCTION

This is another format for doing a poetry explication. In addition to the instruction that attends to that, you would also teach the conventions of interviewing: active listening, piggyback questioning, eye contact and attentive body language, and formulating clear, focused questions.

STANDARDS

In addition to the Standards met by doing a poetry explication, we meet the Standards of effective listening and speaking in this task. Although this is a scripted and rehearsed interview, students have to demonstrate proper social behavior in an interview. In working together to script, rehearse, and perform the interview, students are engaging in purposeful social interaction, focused on a literary subject. Their speech should be free of annoying and immature mannerisms.

CHALLENGE LEVEL

This task requires a mature attitude and the ability to work with a partner. The performance will be as successful as the amount of rehearsal time put into it.. The challenge lies in asking the poem questions that are not obvious and that coax the more subtle meanings of the poem to the surface.

MULTIPLE INTELLIGENCES

This task taps into verbal-linguistic intelligence (analysis of language), interpersonal (working with a partner to write interview questions), and bodily-kinesthetic (exhibiting proper listening behavior in the performance).

SCORING GUIDE

- ◆ Meaning: You've written and presented an interview with a poem that shows insights and analysis and understanding of literary terms.

    4. _____

    3. _____

    2. _____

    1. _____

- ◆ Development: You've discussed various aspects of the poem.

    4. _____

    3. _____

    2. _____

    1. _____

- ◆ Performance: Your performance is polished, showing evidence of rehearsal and planning.

    4. _____

    3. _____

    2. _____

    1. _____

♦ Conventions: Your written script and presentation observe the rules of Standard English (written and oral).

4. _____

3. _____

2. _____

1. _____

FOLLOW-UP

The interview can be used as the pre-writing phase to a more formal poetry explication.

SAMPLE OF STUDENT WORK

ROSS AND TODD: HIGH LEVEL

Script: "A Blessing"

Q: Are you like any other poem that we might know?

A: I might remind you of the Robert Frost poem "Stopping by Woods on a Snowy Evening." In that poem, a man stops on his way home to watch the woods fill up with snow. We have the same themes: getting off the road for a little nature respite; the calming effects of nature.

Q: Why do you call yourself "A Blessing"?

A: The blessing is the peace that the guy gets from stopping his hectic life for a moment to savor the beauty of nature. If you look at my last line, you'll see why I'm called "A Blessing."

Q: I notice the word <u>twilight</u> in your second line. Can you tell me why you use that word rather then, say, the word <u>evening</u> or <u>dusk</u>, which mean almost the same thing?

A: I think 'twilight' is more poetic. It has more light in it than the other words that denote the end of day. 'Evening' is too dark;' dusk' is too hard to say against 'bounds softly'. I just think 'twilight' has the softness that I want here.

Q: The ponies. Are they real or metaphorical?

A: Well, you can certainly think of the ponies as real. But if you wanted to consider them as metaphors for nature in general, I would still make sense and have the same theme. Same with the highway.

Q: I notice a lot of s's. Do you just like this letter or are you trying to say something by repeating it?

A: I alliterate my s's, especially in my closing lines, convey a softness.

Q: What are you trying to get me to think about?

A: I was hoping that you'd think about a time when you got off the highway and took a 'nature break' and enjoyed the simple beauties of nature.

Q: Why did you write yourself?

A: I am trying to evoke the experience of surprise joy that can overtake you when you give in to the beauty of nature and your relationship to God's creatures.

Q: What would you say are your most important words?

A: I think the last line is the most important. I'm expressing the exhilaration that I'm alluding to in all the other lines.

COMMENTARY

Ross and Todd clearly understand the purpose of the task and are able to integrate literary terms (alliteration, theme, metaphor) as well as key verbs (evoke, convey). The script may seem dry, but their delivery was witty and entertaining. They portrayed a deadpan send-up of a Charlie Rose interview.

REMEDIATION

Allow the strongest pairs of students to go first, point out their strengths, and then give weaker students more time to work. Struggling students may need more structure on the interview questions: word banks, sentence stems, model interviews that they can customize to their poems. (Pairing students is always a delicate business. You don't want either party to feel burdened by the other. I usually find it best to allow students to choose their own partners, work with the person sitting next to them, or have a random system.)

FROM POEM TO PROSE

PRODUCT: A PROSE PASSAGE

In this task, students *translate* a poem into prose.

DIRECTIONS TO THE STUDENTS

Act as if you are the poet, but you've decided to write prose instead of poetry. You may keep some of the original words and phrases, while adding enough words to form complete sentences. You may write in the first person or the third person. Your prose piece should convey an understanding of the poem, as well as an understanding of the differences between poetry and prose.

INSTRUCTION

To instruct for this task, you need to illuminate the conventions of poetry and prose. We recognize a poem because of certain conventions of spacing and layout, but what else makes a poem different from prose? What do we expect from a poem and from prose? Can a poem simply be set down as prose, and vice versa?

STANDARDS

The Standards require that students learn to write for different audiences and for a variety of purposes. By translating language from one genre to another, students are analyzing the features of each genre, deciding what to keep and what has to change. This task requires an evaluation of language and making adjustments while retaining the original meaning. Understanding the features of a genre means setting up expectations before reading. We know that when a reader knows what to expect from a text, her comprehension will improve.

CHALLENGE LEVEL

We don't want students to simply copy out the poem as prose. The challenge is to manipulate the language, to adjust it so that it sounds more *prose-like* without sacrificing meaning. Weak students will retain too much of the original language, or will do the opposite, lacking an understanding of key terms and concepts. The consummation devoutly to be wished is that students will begin to use poetic language in their own prose, seeing the value of figurative language in all types of writing.

MULTIPLE INTELLIGENCES

This task requires verbal-linguistic intelligence. Students with strong intrapersonal (understanding of self) skills may wish to write the passage in the first person.

SCORING GUIDE

- ◆ Meaning and Development: You've written a prose piece which retains the meaning of the poem but shows an understanding of the difference between poetry and prose.

    4. _____

    3. _____

    2. _____

    1. _____

- ◆ Organization: You've organized your piece into paragraphs with topic sentences and transition.

    4. _____

    3. _____

    2. _____

    1. _____

- ◆ Conventions: You've observed the rules of spelling, capitalization, punctuation, and presentation.

    4. _____

    3. _____

    2. _____

    1. _____

FOLLOW-UP

Take a prose passage and formulate it into a poem.

SAMPLES OF STUDENT WORK

DAVE: HIGH LEVEL

"A Blessing"
(a retelling of the poem by James Wright)

Sometimes, life's most meaningful experiences are unexpected and amazingly simple. About a year ago, at this time of year, my buddy Mitch and I were riding on the Interstate just outside of Rochester, Minnesota. It was the end of a long day's work, and we were exhausted and stressed out from the day.

We had pulled off the highway to grab a bite of dinner at some fast food place or another, the twilight made the grass sparkle, and we noticed two Indian ponies coming toward us out of the willows. Something about their kind, dark eyes drew us, and, without saying anything, we crossed over the barbed wire into their pasture. They looked happy to see us and they rippled tensely and bowed their heads like wet swans do.

I felt lost in that moment, when they began munching the young tufts of spring as the evening closed in. The smaller one, a black and white pony with a wild mane falling on her forehead, walked over to me and nuzzled my left hand. Her long ear was so soft to the touch, like the skin over my little girl's wrist.

Something about that moment made me forget about whatever had stressed me out that day. I felt no consciousness of myself, as though I had no body. It was one of those rare moments of pure joy, a blessing, when you feel like you could just burst into blossom.

COMMENTARY

Dave embellishes the story without lapsing into too much detail. He shows an excellent understanding of the themes of the poem but integrates the theme into the narrative. He knows when to use the language of the poem, and does so in a natural way. Dave displays the knowledge that poetry is economized language, whereas prose uses more words to sew words together. Note the skillful mention of the title in the last sentence.

CHRISTIAN: MID LEVEL

"A Blessing"
(a retelling of the poem by James Wright)

Just off the highway to Rochester, Minnesota, at twilight, I see the eyes of two Indian ponies. Their eyes darken with kindness and I go over to *them. They look happy to see me and my friend. We step over the barbed wire into the pasture. They have been grazing all day, alone. They look happy to see us. They ripple tensely.*

They bow shyly as wet swans. I think they love each other and that they are lonely. They munch the young tufts of spring in the darkness. I feel like holding the slenderer one in my arms, because she likes me. I know she likes me because she starts nuzzling my hand. She is black and white and has a wild mane over her forehead.

I feel a light breeze and I feel very peaceful here with the ponies. Suddenly I realize that if I stepped out of my body I would break into blossom. I am overjoyed with the wonders of the beautiful scenery and graceful horses that want to be my friends.

COMMENTARY

Christian does have an understanding of the poem on a thematic level, but he uses too much of the poem verbatim without embellishing it to the extent to be expected by a work of prose. Note that the previous student added details to make the piece more story-like. Christian needs to flesh out the story more, using his imagination to fill in unsaid context. The paragraphing here seems a bit random.

SARA: LOW LEVEL

This poem is about two guys who stop off the highway of Rochester, Minnesota to pet some horses. The horses are happy to see them. One of the horses, the slenderer one, is black and white with a wild mane over her forehead. That's the one that nuzzles his left hand....

COMMENTARY

Sara misses the point of the task, lapsing into summary. There's no understanding of theme.

REMEDIATION

It's easier to do this with a poem that conveys a strong narrative. Then, the student can understand that the task is to *retell the story.*

Shakespearean Word Inventory

Product: A List of Words and Phrases Taken from Shakespearean works

In this task, students help themselves to the language of Shakespeare, creating an *inventory* of words and phrases that interest them. They will then use these words/phrases to make their own writing more interesting.

Directions to the Student

The language of Shakespeare is yours to keep. One of the most venerated of literary traditions is to pick through the plays, take what we like, and use it as if it were our own. Doing so is not plagiarism—it is a literary convention known as allusion. If your reader recognizes your phrase as belonging to Shakespeare, then she will consider you educated and enlightened. This task is simple to do: go through one or more of the plays and make a list of words and phrases that appeal to you *and that you think you may use in your writing and/or speech.* Think of this list as an inventory. An inventory is a collection of items that you intend to use. That's exactly what you are going to do with your inventory. You are going to refer to it to light up ideas in your head as you write. Check off your inventory items as you use them. When you use a word or phrase from your list, be sure that it sounds natural and that it suits your context. Keep your inventory in your writing notebook. Many authors use words and phrases from Shakespeare as titles.

Instruction

There are two parts to this task: making the inventory and using it for its intended purpose. The inventory can be categorized or mixed. Categories could be words referring to *nature*, words referring to *emotions*, words referring to the *senses*. Or, you could categorize by grammatical structure: *adjective/noun, prepositional phrases, infinitive phrases.* Students need examples of allusion. Allusions are ubiquitous, but, like taxi cabs on a rainy day, are never around when you need them. Allusions are not catalogued, but when we see a Shakespearean play, we're always saying "So *that's* there that expression comes from!" Make the point that many well-known titles are Shakespearean allusions:

- *The Sound and the Fury*
- *Brave New World*
- *The Quick and the Dead*
- *The Dogs of War*

♦ *Rough Magic*

♦ *What Dreams May Come*

♦ *Outrageous Fortune*

♦ *Something Wicked This Way Comes*

♦ *Remembrance of Things Past*

Students need to know that an allusion to Shakespeare or the Bible should not be attributed to the source. When we quote Shakespeare (or the Bible) we credit our readers with the cultural literacy to recognize the reference without our pointing it out.

Students may want to know the difference between a cliché and an allusion. To use a case in point, the difference lies in the eye of the beholder: Though both cliché and allusion are familiar, the allusion keeps its charm, while, by definition, the cliché has worn out its welcome. An allusion has a literary pedigree and years of experience; the cliché is a parvenu without staying power. Allusions make language sparkle; clichés make it dull.

Give students browse time in their texts. They don't all have to be using the same play. In fact, it works well to spend time picking through one text, then switching. Fifty items is a good start, and students should feel free to add items from each other's lists.

Students will need practice and models to see how they can use the inventory. The key is that the allusion should fit naturally into the sentence. It shouldn't look as though you've inserted a bit of Shakespeare just to be pretentious. For practice, ask students to describe an aspect of nature or a month of the year, using an item from their inventory:

> "…and, for the first time that year, I heard the stiff and stark voice of winter."

Here, the phrase *stiff and stark* is lifted from *Romeo and Juliet*.

Hundreds of well-known and colorful expressions originate in Shakespeare's plays, such as *hit or miss, bag and baggage, flesh and blood, word and deed, cold comfort, foul play, tower of strength, vanish into thin air, play fast and loose,* and *wild goose chase.*

STANDARDS

This task is about the poetry and richness of the English language. It addresses the Standard of understanding how literary elements add meaning, beauty and nuance to a written work. Because many of the items in the inventory will themselves be figures of speech and will display euphony (alliteration, assonance, onomatopoeia), learning to keep and use an inventory teaches these techniques.

MULTIPLE INTELLIGENCES

Submitting oneself to the joy of words and welcoming new words into one's vocabulary requires verbal-linguistic intelligence. Since the language of Shakespeare (and all poetry, for that matter) is visual, musical, sensuous, and emotional, students who excel in the nonverbal intelligences should do well in this task.

CHALLENGE LEVEL

Ironically enough, the challenge of this task lies in understanding how easy it is to do. If students are laboriously searching for just the right phrase to include in their inventories, if they are crossing out and going through page after page with little fruit, then they need to loosen up. The idea is to place words and phrase into one's shopping cart with no particular thought as to their eventual use. When we have such words listed in profusion, then they will trigger ideas in our later writings.

SCORING GUIDE

This scoring guide applies to the inventory itself, not to the use of the words/phrases in the student's own writing. Use of such words is reflected in the *word choice* category in other rubrics. Although the use of Shakespearean allusions is to be encouraged, it is a mistake to require it on a regular basis, because doing so would sound forced.

Check One

_____ Your inventory is:

        _____ interesting

        _____ thorough

        _____ varied

_____ You have:

        _____ many

        _____ a few words here that you can use in your own writing and speech.

_____ You've chosen words and phrases that will probably have limited application to your own writing and speech.

_____ Your inventory is incomplete.

FOLLOW-UP

Keeping an inventory of words (aka word journal) is a powerful habit of mind. A student who has this will never be at a loss for words. The inventory can be expanded to include all kinds of sources: poetry, the Bible, newspapers (film, music, sports, and food sections are great sources). Once students have at least 100 words/phrases, you can categorize them in various ways. Doing so keeps the inventory in the students' consciousness.

SAMPLES OF STUDENT WORK

MEGGIE: HIGH LEVEL

The following list is taken from <u>The Comedy of Errors</u>, <u>Twelfth Night</u>, *and* <u>Othello</u>.

> *venom*
> *a mad dog's tooth*
> *had I the heart to do it*
> *point of death*
> *tempests*
> *savage jealousy*
> *my true place in your favor*
> *marble-breasted tyrant*
> *fool's paradise*
> *fortune's fool*
> *outward character*
> *watery tomb*
> *'Tis a pageant to keep us in false gaze*
> *profitless*
> *a danger profitless*
> *warlike brace*
> *to please the palate of my appetite*

COMMENTARY

Note that some of these phrases are already well known; others are almost whole sentences; others, single words. This is a successful inventory because Meggie has chosen words that are not so exotic or Shakespearean that they can't be worked in to ordinary language.

KAYLA: MID LEVEL

light-winged toys
with wanton dullness
a moth of peace
let housewives make a skillet of my helm
quench the guards
the foaming shore
in full commission

COMMENTARY

Although Kayla has interesting phrases here, it's doubtful that they will serve much practical use to her in her ordinary writing and speech, unless she is writing about a Shakespearean play. But the purpose of the inventory is not just to write about Shakespeare. It is to enrich one's language on all subjects.

NICOLETTE: LOW LEVEL

present me as an eunuch to him
I'll serve this duke
The chidden billow
on the enchafed flood
But this same Cassio
Good ancient, you are welcome.

COMMENTARY

Nicolette is even less likely than Kayla to use these terms, which are far too specific to their contexts to apply to general subjects. You get the feeling that she chose these terms at random, without giving much thought to their selection.

REMEDIATION

Students who don't see the point of the inventory should be encouraged to write no more than three word phrases. Then, you can assign particular descriptive topics that would lend themselves to the use of these phrases. Good ones are: *night, morning, winter, summer, a month of the year.*

SUMMARY

The performance tasks in this chapter teach students how to read the subtle levels of poetry, identify poetic devices, and explain their effects on meaning. These are reading comprehension skills that further understanding of other literature that employs figurative language. These tasks can be applied to simple as well as complex poetry, and are particularly suited to modern lyric poems.

8

PERFORMANCE TASKS BASED ON SYNTAX

CHAPTER OVERVIEW

The performance tasks in this chapter use grammatical concepts to improve sentence-writing skills. Meaning is conveyed at the level of the sentence. Time spent teaching students how to structure a sturdy sentence is time spent teaching them how to organize and build their thoughts. In other words, sentence grammar dictates and organizes information flow.

Without explicit knowledge of grammar, we limit our ability to reflect on and control what we say. True literacy involves reflection on language—the ability to evaluate and change not only our word choice but also our word order, sentence combinations, punctuation varieties, and subordination.

One thing we need to realize is that writing professional-sounding sentences, that is to say, writing sentences that embed subordinate elements, is largely a matter of linguistic development. Linguists tell us that students are ready to generate sentences containing embedded and reduced subordinate elements in the tenth grade or so. Before that, they are simply not ready for the kinds of sentences that sound professional.

This section consists of these performance tasks:

- ◆ Recipe for an Essay: Sentence Structure Ingredients
- ◆ Syntax and Active Reading Techniques
- ◆ Emphasis
- ◆ Building Suspense by Postponing the Subject
- ◆ Punctuation Analysis
- ◆ Thinking in Verbs

RECIPE FOR AN ESSAY:
SENTENCE STRUCTURE INGREDIENTS

PRODUCT: AN ESSAY OF EXPOSITORY WRITING

This task reverses the revision project, but it accomplishes the same thing. Instead of writing the draft and then revising for given structures, the recipe calls for these structures up front. The student writes the essay with these structures in mind.

DIRECTIONS TO THE STUDENTS

Write an essay on a topic of your choice that displays the following grammatical structures:

- Three different kinds of parallel structure

- Four complex sentences

- One pair of appositive adjectives

- Two sentences that contain interruptive elements

- Two sentences that contain contrasting ideas

SYNTAX AND ACTIVE
READING TECHNIQUES

Although we usually think of syntax instruction in relation to writing, we can use an awareness of syntax to boost reading comprehension as well. We surely know that we improve reading comprehension when these conditions are met:

- The reader recognizes that certain words signal certain organizational patterns;

- The reader is engaged in the text: asking questions, taking notes, stopping at intervals to summarize;

- The reader brings prior knowledge and expectations to the text;

- The reading material has textual features, such as headings, subheadings, columns, and a variety of type sizes that break up the page and cue the reader as to what's important;

- the reader understands the vocabulary or can figure it out through contextual clues.

In addition, we know that schemata such as graphic organizers are important comprehension aids. We also know that good readers approach a reading task with a variety of strategies and that they adjust their reading rates according to the purpose and the content. Good readers have a metacognitive awareness of their own strengths and needs as readers.

Many of the conditions necessary for optimal reading comprehension require the reader to perceive organizational patterns in text. Because syntax is all about organization, it stands to reason that knowledge of how sentences are put together can be a tool for comprehension.

PRODUCT: THREE SENTENCES PER PAGE OF TEXT

In this task, students select one verb (or verb phrase), one noun (or noun phrase) and one adjective (or adjective phrase) from a given page of text, and explain the significance of these words to the meaning of the text as a whole.

DIRECTIONS TO THE STUDENTS

You will be a better reader if you reflect on what you read as you go along. One way to reflect is to consider why the writer has chosen certain words. Take one page of text and consider one verb, one noun and one adjective. Select words from different parts of the page. For each, write a sentence that explains the meaning of these words in the context of the writer's message as a whole. This task accomplishes the following:

- ♦ It will get you to think about what is most important in the text.

- ♦ It will show you how a writer uses verbs, nouns, and adjectives to convey meaning and tone.

- ♦ It will help you review.

- ♦ It will serve as a word bank for any writing that you might do about this material.

INSTRUCTION

This task may require a review about parts of speech and about the fact that a given word can play different parts of speech, depending upon context. If we were to ask for any three words, rather than a verb, a noun, and an adjective, students wouldn't be considering the text from as wide an angle as they do when we ask for these three parts of speech.

Why is this word important to the meaning? We are asking for more than just what the word means. What does it imply? Evoke? How does it express the author's theme and how does it have a meaning beyond this particular sentence and page?

CHALLENGE LEVEL

This task requires higher-level thinking because, in selecting words, the student has to evaluate the impact of some words over others. Which words carry the most weight in what the author is trying to convey?

SCORING GUIDE

- ◆ Meaning: You've explained how a verb, a noun, and an adjective from different parts of the page convey the author's meaning.

    4. _____

    3. _____

    2. _____

    1. _____

- ◆ Word Choice: You've selected words that best convey the meaning of the piece as a whole.

    4. _____

    3. _____

    2. _____

    1. _____

- ◆ Conventions: You've followed the rules of spelling, punctuation, capitalization, and sentence structure.

    4. _____

    3. _____

    2. _____

    1. _____

FOLLOW-UP

Students can use their ideas to write fully developed thematic essays. They can also turn this process back on their own writing, explaining their own word choices in the context of a theme in expository or creative writing.

OTHER SYNTACTICAL TECHNIQUES

As students learn to apply the techniques above, they can focus on other syntactical techniques. We can approach almost all rhetorical improvements from a syntactical strategy.

♦ To achieve vivid sensual detail, sharpen your nouns. Comb through your piece and identify nouns that could be made more specific. Instead of saying *I had many problems on the ice*, say what the problems were: *I couldn't spin around fast enough. My blades flattened out on the ice and my knees collapsed under me.*

♦ To be more concise, downsize your modifier force. Many adjectives are superfluous. There is no sense in saying that the *green hillside* was dotted with *purple violets*, or that the shocking news was *unexpected*. If the noun already contains the concept, then we can eliminate the modifier, or find one that actually modifies the noun or verb.

♦ To achieve variety in sentence beginnings, start some sentences with prepositional phrases, some with participial phrases, and some with modifiers.

♦ To achieve clarity and gracefulness, use a variety of punctuation marks. Punctuation is to the written word what tone of voice is to the spoken word.

EMPHASIS

Writers strive for clarity. One way of achieving clarity is by placing the emphasis where we want it in a sentence, a paragraph, or an essay. We can control the emphasis in a sentence by understanding how syntax affects meaning.

PRODUCT: THREE SENTENCES REPRESENTING DIFFERENT SYNTACTICAL VERSIONS OF THE SAME SET OF EVENTS

In this task, students will show that they understand how a given set of events gets different emphasis, depending upon word order and subordination.

DIRECTIONS TO THE STUDENTS

The purpose of this task is to show you how to write sentences so that the emphasis is where you want it. Write a sentence that could appear in a fairy tale or legend, and then rewrite it several times, changing the emphasis by using various rhetorical techniques. Your sentence should have at least three events going on, so that you can move them around. Label each sentence with the technique that it demonstrates.

INSTRUCTION

First, some theory: In the English language, there are several syntactic conventions that result in emphasis of a particular sentence element:

- ♦ Position

    The emphasized element can be placed up front, for immediate recognition, or it can be placed at the end of the sentence, as a crescendo.

- ♦ Word choice

    A writer may choose words of greater or lesser intensity to show where the emphasis is supposed to be.

- ♦ Punctuation

    Most writing teachers discourage exclamation points, preferring more subtle methods of achieving emphasis, but we can also use a colon to lead up to and point out the empahatic part of the sentence.

- ♦ Textual features

    Obvious textual features such as boldface, italics, bulleted lists, and capital letters signal emphasis.

- ♦ Interruptive elements

    In informal writing, the writer often inserts commentary set off by dashes to direct the emphasis.

In addition to these conventions, students need to understand how subordination dictates emphasis. That is to say: what we want emphasized should be in the main clause, not the subordinate clause. Consider the sentence: *When James asked Marcia to marry him, they were dining on chow fun noodles in a little takeout place near Hoboken.*

If we want the proposal emphasized here, then we shouldn't bury it in a subordinate clause. More effective syntax would place James' proposal in the main clause, either at the beginning or at the end of the sentence, as in the following examples: *James asked Marcia to marry him while they were dining on chow fun noodles in a little takeout place near Hoboken;* or *While they were dining on chow fun noodles in a little takeout place near Hoboken, James asked Marcia to marry him.*

Students need to understand the following grammatical concepts to do this task:

♦ Main clause (aka independent clause)

♦ Subordinate clause (aka dependent clause)

SCORING GUIDE

♦ Meaning and Development: Your sentences and labels indicate that you understand how different rhetorical techniques can change the emphasis.

4. _____

3. _____

2. _____

1. _____

♦ Word Choice: Your vocabulary is interesting and appropriate to the tone of the story.

4. _____

3. _____

2. _____

1. _____

♦ Presentation: You've observed the rules of spelling, capitalization, and punctuation and your paper is neat and easy to follow.

4. _____

3. _____

2. _____

1. _____

FOLLOW-UP

We can apply this skill to reading comprehension as well as to writing. When students develop an awareness of the syntactical signals that cue emphasis, they can become more efficient readers, because they know where to look for the important parts of meaning. What we've also established in this task is that effective writing consists of a variety of factors: position, subordination, word choice, punctuation, and textual features.

SAMPLE OF STUDENT WORK

BRIAN: HIGH LEVEL

Word order/subordination: (The emphasized parts are underlined)

1. When the clock struck twelve, <u>Cinderella ran down the palace steps</u> and dropped her slipper.

2. <u>Cinderella dropped her slipper</u> when she ran down the palace steps as the clock struck twelve.

3. <u>As the clock struck twelve,</u> Cinderella ran down the palace steps and dropped her slipper.

Using a colon:

4. The clock struck twelve and here's what happened: <u>Cinderella ran down the palace steps and dropped her slipper.</u>

Using an interrupter:

5. The clock struck twelve and Cinderella ran down the palace steps and—in her panic—<u>she dropped her slipper.</u>

Textual features:

6. When the clock struck twelve, Cinderella ran down the palace steps and <u>dropped her slipper.</u>

Word choice:

7. When the clock struck twelve, Cinderella <u>flew</u> down the palace steps and dropped her slipper.

COMMENTARY

The student who wrote the model above was able to generate the seven techniques himself; a less able student would have to be given these techniques and asked to write sentences for them.

BUILDING SUSPENSE BY POSTPONING THE SUBJECT

Building suspense by postponing the subject is a popular and effective technique for literary writing. Another name for such sentences is the *periodic sentence*.

PRODUCT: A LITERARY SENTENCE

In this task, students write a sentence that builds suspense by postponing the subject.

DIRECTIONS TO THE STUDENTS

Writers, especially writers of fiction, often use a technique in which they postpone the subject of the sentence until the end. The purpose of this technique is to build suspense by having the subject make a grand entrance. Think of a fairy tale or legend and write three sentences (about the same thing) that use different grammatical elements before the subject appears.

INSTRUCTION

Students have to understand that the first noun that they encounter in the sentence is not necessarily the subject. This means explaining or reviewing the fact that the object of a preposition is not the subject. The periodic sentence often establishes a series, and is therefore an opportunity to teach or review parallel structure. Show several models, illustrating various grammatical constructions that are effective in the periodic sentence.

Students do not necessarily need the term *periodic sentence*, but they do need the following terms: *subject, verb, phrase, clause.*

CHALLENGE LEVEL

The challenge is for students to see that the words preceding the subject are phrases, not clauses. Yes, they can write wonderful sentences without following this restriction, but the point of the task is to understand the sentence on a syntactical level.

FOLLOW-UP

The reverse of this pattern, where accumulating details follow the subject, is useful in descriptive writing: *Cinderella wept, thinking about the many miserable chores that lay ahead: folding the laundry, ironing the petticoats, dusting the little statuettes on her stepsisters' bureaus.*

SAMPLE OF STUDENT WORK

ZOE: HIGH LEVEL

1. All alone and left to do household chores like folding laundry, dusting furniture, and polishing candlesticks, <u>Cinderella wept</u>.

2. *Feeling disheveled, unglamorous, and utterly forsaken, <u>Cinderella wept</u>.*

3. *Having abandoned hope for an invitation to the ball, <u>Cinderella wept</u>.*

REMEDIATION

When students can't discern the subject of a sentence, the problem is usually that they don't recognize prepositional phrases. They can write a sentence that includes a subject at the end, but they haven't met the requirements of the task, and their sentence won't have the desired impact. One method of remediation is to have students cross out all prepositional phrases before looking for the subject.

PUNCTUATION ANALYSIS

PRODUCT: ANNOTATIONS OF TEXT EXPLAINING PUNCTUATION USE

In this task, students write notations on text, explaining, in grammatical terms, why they use given marks of punctuation.

DIRECTIONS TO THE STUDENTS

Find a text in a newspaper, magazine, or literature that uses various marks of punctuation. Type or handwrite the text, double-spaced and with wide margins. You should have one page to work with. Explain, using grammatical terms, why you've used each mark of punctuation. Write your explanations directly on the page of text.

INSTRUCTION

Novice writers often have vague ideas about the rules of punctuation. They think that they are supposed to use commas to signal a pause, but that notion doesn't really guide them when it comes to their own writing. Novices seldom use marks of punctuation other than a comma or a period, yet professional writers make use of a much wider variety for interesting effects, voice, and tone. To do this task, students will need to use grammatical terms such as appositive, restrictive/nonrestrictive elements, independent clause, and so on. Students should do this task by working with a grammar book that explains the rules of punctuation use.

CHALLENGE LEVEL

The first challenge is to select appropriate text for this task and then to reproduce it accurately. Then, students have to employ grammatical terminology, rather than saying "there's a pause here." The explanations have to be succinct, as marginal notes.

SCORING GUIDE

- ♦ Choice of Text:
  - • Suitable for this task _____
  - • Unsuitable for this task _____
- ♦ Annotations:
  - • Explained adequately _____
  - • Not explained adequately _____
  - • Grammatical terms not used _____
  - • Explanations incorrect _____
  - • Omissions _____

FOLLOW-UP

The annotation technique can identify other grammatical structures found in text. Students can compare and contrast pages of text by the same author, or on a single subject by different authors, and draw conclusions about how punctuation and syntax affect ease of reading.

THINKING IN VERBS

PRODUCT: A PARAGRAPH CHARACTER SKETCH

In this task, students write a one-paragraph character sketch in which they use verbs to show that a character displays particular character traits set forth as adjectives.

DIRECTIONS TO THE STUDENTS

When you read literature, you draw conclusions about characters based on what they do, how others speak about them, and what the author tells you. A character sketch includes adjectives, such as the ones below, that describe personality traits. Once you perceive that a character displays a given trait, you must justify your assertion by giving examples of actions (expressed in verbs) that the character does. Write a one-paragraph character sketch that justifies your assertions by giving specific examples of actions (verbs) that the character does in the story.

Character Traits

Positive

animated	adventurous	analytical	adaptable
persistent	playful	persuasive	peaceful
submissive	self-sacrificing	sociable	strong-willed
considerate	controlled	competitive	convincing
refreshing	respectful	reserved	resourceful
satisfied	sensitive	self-reliant	spirited
patient	confident	spontaneous	friendly
disciplined	tenacious	loyal	bouncy
talkative	decisive	deep	humorous
diplomatic	inoffensive	sympathetic	demonstrative
vivacious	contented	meditative	shy
optimistic	inspiring	productive	wise

Negative

bossy	undisciplined	unsympathetic	unenthusiastic
unforgiving	reluctant	fussy	impatient
negative	insistent	vengeful	sluggish
irresponsible	stubborn	restless	sneaky
indifferent	alienated	cold	selfish
arrogant	lazy	argumentative	nervy
hard to please	flippant	insecure	resentful
jealous	cynical	pessimistic	

INSTRUCTION

To do this task, students need to make inferences based on literature. They need to consider the textual evidence available through various sources: a character's own speech and actions, how others view the character, and what the narrator says directly about the character. The above list is to suggest, but not to limit, character traits.

STANDARDS

This task meets the Standard that calls for being able to interpret literature and justify assertions.

CHALLENGE LEVEL

The challenge level depends upon how perceptive the inferences are. Some students will state the obvious about a character, while others will show insight into more subtle elements of human behavior. Much about character behavior and its significance comes to light upon a second reading, when the reader notices foreshadowing that he missed the first time around.

MULTIPLE INTELLIGENCES

In addition to the linguistic skills that go into writing the paragraph, this task requires interpersonal intelligence to make judgments and inferences about human behavior.

SCORING GUIDE

- ◆ Meaning: You've written a one paragraph character sketch that justifies with verbs the assertions that you've made with adjectives.

    4. _____

    3. _____

    2. _____

    1. _____

- ◆ Development: You've given at least two character traits and at least two examples of behavior for each.

    4. _____

    3. _____

    2. _____

    1. _____

- ◆ Organization: Your paragraph has a topic sentence and supportive sentences, presented in a logical order.

    4. _____

    3. _____

    2. _____

    1. _____

♦ Word choice: Your vocabulary is interesting, varied, and appropriate

   4. _____

   3. _____

   2. _____

   1. _____

♦ Conventions: You've followed the conventions of spelling, capitalization, sentence structure, and presentation.

   4. _____

   3. _____

   2. _____

   1. _____

FOLLOW-UP

The frame of mind here, using verbs to justify assertions made by adjectives, applies to all subjects. Adjective-to-verb thinking applies to social studies: If we assert that *Japan is technologically advanced*, then we need to justify that assertion by saying *what Japan produces*. It also applies to science: We can say that *friction causes inefficiency in a car's engine* but we don't show an understanding of that statement until we think in verbs. What do ball bearings and lubrication *do to reduce friction* and *maximize efficiency*? We can approach a question by refining the verbs that apply to it. What do enzymes *do*? They *break down* food in the digestive system. How? They *accelerate* the chemical changes that transform sugar into glucose.

SAMPLES OF STUDENT WORK

JULIA: HIGH LEVEL

> To Kill A Mockingbird by Harper Lee is narrated by Scout, a spunky schoolgirl. Scout rebels against the adult women who play stand-in mothers to her. She refuses to wear dresses, except when she has to. She gets into fights to defend her father, who is a defense lawyer in a controversial trial. Scout is precocious. She knows how to read before she begins school. She learned to read by sitting on her father's lap while he read the newspaper. Every chapter in the novel presents a lesson in life to Scout.

COMMENTARY

Note the sturdy structure of this paragraph: a strong topic sentence and a concluding sentence hold it together. The stuff of the paragraph supports the assertions that Scout is *spunky* and *precocious*. The sentences flow naturally from one to the other. (Note also the proper use of conventions in referring to literature in the first sentence.)

PAUL: MID LEVEL

To Kill a Mockingbird is a story about racism in the South. It stars Atticus Finch, a lawyer who is defending a black man against the charge of raping a white woman. Atticus is serious and protecting. We know that he is serious because he makes the children read to there neighbor when she taunts at them. Also because he tells Scout not to fight if anyone teases her at school at the relatives. He does not brag that he has dead eye aim. He only uses it for emergencies like when a rabid dog comes down the block. He is protecting of Scout and Jem not wanting them to come down the courthouse. He knows there are people in the town who would harm them because of what he has done.

COMMENTARY

This student understands the task and the character, but his unskilled writing style diminishes his message. (Note the use of *protecting* for *protective*.)

Elyse: Low Level

To Kill a Mockingbird is about a black man whose accused of raping a white woman. But she falsely accuses him. Mayella Ewell is white trash she lives with Bob Ewell her father and alot of children. The children were not on the place when the supposed rape took place. The place was really crappy, Mayella asks Tom to come in and bust up a chiffarobe and then she throws her arms around him. That's when her father comes along and the false accusation begins. Tom is the black man who is accused of raping a white girl.

COMMENTARY

Well, we have plenty of action verbs here but we have no clear assertion of character traits. This student lapses into summary rather than addressing the task. (Note the inappropriate diction.)

REMEDIATION

When a weak student has to answer a question about literature and he does not understand what the question is asking him to do, he lapses into summary. Such students need to work with outlines and graphic organizers so that they can see the difference between referring to events in the story, to make a point, and summarizing the story.

SUMMARY

The tasks presented in this chapter get students to use grammatical terms to better express themselves. If we teach grammatical terms in this integrated way, and if the student sees immediate rhetorical benefit to using the terms they've just learned, then the instruction is effective. But there is much agreement that the method of teaching grammatical terms in isolation, by the discredited *drill and kill* method, are ineffective.

When we teach grammar in the context of a performance task, we eliminate the frustrating problem of having students perform well on grammar tests but failing to apply what they've learned to their writing.

Sentence combining, mini-lessons, analysis and correction of student-written sentences, and modeling of professional sentences are some of the methods for improving writing through explicit grammar instruction. The performance tasks shown here should be supplemented with such methods.

Terminology is powerful. With the language of the language, we can teach students about the options that are available to them such as:

♦ Sentence variety maintains reader interest

♦ Postponing the subject builds suspense

♦ Parallel sentence structure facilitates reading and causes the prose to be memorable

♦ Using conjunctions facilitates comprehension

Simply telling students such information has limited impact. What does have impact is pointing out these principles in real text, whether written by the students themselves or by professionals.

This method of grammar instruction recognizes two important facets of learning about language. The first is that learning grammar has a purpose that goes beyond correcting errors. Its purpose is to show students what they can do inside a sentence and how grammar relates to style. The second facet of language that the revision project recognizes is that grammar instruction has to be immediately applicable to one's own writing. Workbook grammar has long been discredited and many computer-assisted grammar tutorials are not much more than onscreen workbooks. The revision project fuses the learning of traditional terminology with sentence combining, resulting in improved writing that we can measure when we compare the baseline to the revision.

9

PERFORMANCE TASKS BASED ON LITERARY CRITICISM

CHAPTER OVERVIEW

Students often misunderstand the term *literary criticism:* they apply the vernacular definition of *criticism*, thinking it means only to *find fault with*. Yet, they do need to understand the term in its literary context because the evaluative thinking involved in literary criticism is an important form of higher-level learning.

Literary criticism is the analysis, interpretation, and evaluation of a work of literature against criteria. There are various schools and systems of literary criticism, such as *classic* (evaluating a work against universal aesthetic principles), *deconstructionist* (exposing multiple meanings in text), *affective* (basing judgment on emotional response), *historical* (judging the historical accuracy), and *structural* (judging whether or not the author has put the parts of the story together logically and brought it to a close).

Students need to realize that writing literary criticism is not necessarily the same as writing a critique or review. The key to what literary criticism is all about is *establishing criteria and then judging the literature against them.*

What that in mind, the following performance tasks show students how to participate in literary criticism:

♦ Judging Literary Merit

♦ Critical Lens

♦ Proposing a Book for Summer Reading

Judging Literary Merit

Product: Essay

In this task, students will write a five-paragraph essay in which they judge the literary merit of a novel against given criteria.

Directions to Students

Write a five-paragraph essay in which you evaluate the literary merit of a book that you have read from our list. Use the suggested criteria given below or you may wish to include other criteria in your evaluation. You may combine or omit criteria as you see fit. Be sure to refer to specific characters and events.

- ◆ Characterization

  Are the characters memorable? Can you picture them clearly? Are their actions consistent with what the author leads you to expect? Do you care about these characters and about how the plot affects them? Are the characters multifaceted, or are they stereotypical and shallow?

- ◆ Theme

  Is the book about something important? Does it cause you to think about human nature, life, the world, history, or other people?

- ◆ Style

  Is the writing engaging? Does the language flow naturally? Are the words and phrases interesting? Are there sentences and passages that you want to read over again?

- ◆ Plot

  Is the story interesting? Does it make sense? Does it have surprises? Irony? Suspense? Are there subplots? Does the story take you on interesting side trips?

- ◆ Setting

  Do you feel as though you've visited another place and time? Can you picture the setting clearly? Is there enough detail? Do vivid images stand out in your mind? Does the book give you insight into history?

♦ Overall Impression

Did the book broaden your knowledge? Make you think? Touch your emotions? Make you feel like laughing or crying? Would you recommend it to a friend? Does the story have a richer meaning as you reflect on it? Does the meaning of the title change as you think about it? Would you get more out of this book if you were to read it again? Is the subject something that you already know about and have some connection to?

INSTRUCTION

It was good because I liked it. I liked it because it was cool.
I didn't like it because it was stupid. It was stupid because it was boring.

We'd like our students to express their views of literature more articulately than this. The fact is, they may not know how. We need to give them the language that they will need to justify their literary taste. They must ground their opinion, valid as it may be, in some sort of criteria. We need to give them the language and tell them the aspects of literature that they might want to consider.

High school students also need to be coaxed away from the idea that a book has to be easy to read in order to be *good*. Serious literature elevates the reader and demands skill, patience, concentration, and an open mind.

And, as always, we have to establish the fact that a response to a question about literary merit does not call for summary. We need to show models that illustrate this difference.

Finally, we need to declare a moratorium on *shut down* words in discussing literature. These are words, such as *boring* and *stupid* that preclude insightful discussion. In discourse that is supposed to be analytical, interpretative, and evaluative, dismissive words, such as *boring* and *stupid,* just won't get us anywhere.

STANDARDS

In this task, we require students to apply reading strategies, both literal and inferential, to improve and demonstrate their understanding. They need to refer to the features of a given genre and tell whether or not the literature displays the expected qualities of the genre. They need to perceive tone and voice in literature and, often, appreciate the use of non-standard dialect. Formal standard written English is required.

CHALLENGE LEVEL

The challenge level varies depending on the nature of the literature and the student's familiarity with it and with the genre of literary criticism.

SCORING GUIDE

- ◆ Meaning: You've shown how the literature measures up against appropriate criteria.

    4. _____

    3. _____

    2. _____

    1. _____

- ◆ Development: You've discussed various aspects of the book and made specific references to literary elements of it; you've referred to various criteria.

    4. _____

    3. _____

    2. _____

    1. _____

- ◆ Organization: You've written well-developed paragraphs with appropriate transition, introduction and conclusion.

    4. _____

    3. _____

    2. _____

    1. _____

- ◆ Word Choice: Your vocabulary is interesting, varied, and appropriate for literary criticism. Your sentence structure is varied, concise and clear.

    4. _____

    3. _____

    2. _____

    1. _____

♦ Presentation: You've observed the rules of standard written English: spelling, punctuation, capitalization, and sentence structure.

4. _____

3. _____

2. _____

1. _____

FOLLOW-UP

As their abilities develop, students should be able to write longer essays of literary criticism, compare and contrast, as well as discern the distinctions in different systems of literary criticism.

SAMPLES OF STUDENT WORK

SHARI: HIGH LEVEL

Essay of Literary Merit
Snow Falling on Cedars by David Guterson

After reading David Guterson's Snow Falling on Cedars, I went out and bought another novel that he wrote, called East of the Mountains. Cedars is the kind of book that you can't stop thinking about. It's a murder trial, a war story and a love story, but it's also a story of a chapter of American history that is very disturbing: the internment of Japanese Americans during World War II.

Cedars portrays characters who are caught up in terrible circumstances. Kabuo Miyamoto is on trial for the murder of his fellow fisherman, Carl Heine. Kabuo's family had lost their strawberry farmland because they were sent to the internment camp at Manzanar. Kabuo is married to the beautiful heroine, Hatsue. Before the war, when she was a teenager, she was in love with Ishmael Chambers, and he was in love with her, but her mother disapproved of him because of the racial differences and she married Kabuo in Manzanar. My heart broke for Ishmael when he reads her "Dear John" letter. Later in the war he loses his arm and his broken heart for Hatsui never repairs. He returns to the small fishing island as a journalist and is now covering the murder story of the husband of the woman he has always loved.

Cedars begins with the horrible news of the drowning death of a popular fisherman named Carl Heine. Carl, a father of two small children, drowned on his fishing boat under suspicious circumstances that lead to the arrest of Kabuo. The author spares us no details in describing the discovery of Carl's body and what happens in the aftermath.

One interesting aspect of the book is the way the story goes back and forth between the night of the drowning, the trial, the years before the war, and during the war. All of these parts are like stories within a story. You get lost in the strawberry fields, the battleground, and the sea. In the end, you realize that the title, which sounds pretty unexciting, refers to things you can't control, like the weather, and things that you can control. When Ishmael does some investigating at the lighthouse, he's looking for information about the weather, but what he finds ends up exonerating an innocent man. That's something that Ishmael can control, and, in the end, though it means that he will never have the love of his life, he does control Kabuo's fate.

I like it when a book feels like a whole world, and Snow Falling on Cedars gave me this feeling. I felt like it was many books put together.

COMMENTARY

Shari has discerned that literary criticism is not a book report in which we don't want to reveal the ending, nor is it an answer to a closed-end question, nor is it a presentation of *my favorite parts* of a book. She has judged the book in terms of character, theme, description, historical significance, and symbolism. Shari has given us her personal response, but it is based on valid literary criteria. What her tone lacks in professionalism, she makes up for in sincerity.

SAM: MID LEVEL

Essay of Literary Merit
Snow Falling on Cedars by David Guterson

Snow Falling on Cedars is about a murder trial and a love story. It takes place on San Piedro Island which is in the state of Washington. The time is the early 1950s a few years after World War II.

Circumstantial evidence leads the town to believe that a Japanese American man named Kabuo killed a fisherman named Carl Heine by hitting him over the head and dropping his body in the water.

The story has irony because the journalist, a man named Ishmael Chambers, is not looking for evidence about the trial but he finds exonerating evidence when he is looking for information about the storm. The storm is why the story has the title <u>Snow Falling on Cedars.</u> That is what you can't control. What you can and can't control is a theme of this book because Ishmael was in love with Hatsue and he could not control that her mother made her break up with him because he was not Japanese.

The characters are very real in this book. Carl Heine seems like a very decent guy but his mother is harsh to the Miyamoto family and sells land that they thought they were getting to another farmer. The characters are not stereotyped but Kabuo is treated as a stereotype because he is un-emotional at his trial. His officer says he is capable of murder because he had certain martial arts skills that the Japanese were known to have. But Kabuo was an innocent man. It was just circumstantial evidence.

This book makes you feel like you've been there. The war parts are very graphic especially when Ishmael loses his arm in the war and in the operating room he sees his amputated arm on a pile in the corner with the fingers curled up. I will never forget that.

The end of the book is poignant. Meaning that it is bittersweet when Kabuo is exonerated but Carl Heine is still dead and Ishmael is still alone and can never have the woman he loves, Hatsue.

COMMENTARY

Although Sam lacks stylistic sophistication and the paragraphs go astray of their topic sentences, she does adhere to literary criteria and shows an understanding of the task as well as key points of the book. She speaks of characterization, theme, and his emotional response. The use of the words *poignant* and *exoneration* seem a bit stilted, but are used correctly. We assume that these were words stressed by the teacher, as they are key to the plot line and emotional impact of this book.

ESTHER: LOW LEVEL

<u>Essay of Literary Merit</u>
<u>Snow Falling on Cedars</u> by David Guterson

No one who lives on San Piedro Island can afford to make enemies. It is a small fishing island off the coast of Puget Sound in Washington. In 1954 a local fisherman is found drowned and the town is suspicious. They accuse a man named Kabuo Miyamoto of the crime and charge him with murder. From there the story goes on to say that everybody has there memories of the dead man and the accused murderer.

San Piedro is haunted by the memory of what happened years ago during the War. This book is gripping, tragic, and densely atmospheric. It is considered a masterpiece of suspense. I thought it was too long.

COMMENTARY

Perhaps Esther tried to read the book but didn't know how to focus on it. . This is information that is gleaned from promotional material, such as the book jacket or quick Internet reviews.

REMEDIATION

The first, and most difficult course of remediation, is to get the students to read the book. Reluctant readers can sometimes be seduced into reading a good book if their peers recommend one. Students should know their reading rates and establish a *reading budget*, setting aside a realistic amount of time per day to get the assigned number of pages read. And the reading task should be scaffolded. Some effective scaffolding techniques that help students with a long reading task are:

- Story outlines
- Graphic organizers
- Study guides
- Historical background
- Character sketches
- Small group discussion
- Visuals, including movies
- Similar stories
- Close looks at key passages
- Reading aloud (by a skillful reader)
- Reader response journals
- Projects that are done concurrently with reading
- Having a reading partner

CRITICAL LENS ESSAY

In what is known as the *critical lens* essay, the student evaluates literature against the criteria implied by a quotation. The quotation is called the *critical lens*.

PRODUCT: A LITERARY ESSAY

In this task, students write an essay that interprets a critical quotation about literature, establishes criteria implied by the quotation, and then supports or refutes the validity of the quotation by referring to two works of literature.

DIRECTIONS TO THE STUDENTS

A good book should serve as an ax to the frozen sea within us.

Franz Kafka

Write an essay in which you interpret this quotation and tell whether or not you agree with it as you've interpreted it. Establish criteria that a book would have to meet in order to support or refute this quotation. Select two works of literature and show how they support or refute the quotation. Be sure to give specific references to the literature.

INSTRUCTION

The term *critical lens* can't just fly in from nowhere. Students need to be familiar with this term, and consider it a genre of essay writing that has certain features. When a student sees the words *critical lens,* the student should be thinking:

- I have to say what the quotation means to me. (I may have to define some of the terms—not a dictionary definition, but my own definition.)

- I have to agree or disagree with what I've said it means.

- I have to say what a work of literature would have to do in order to support or refute this quotation.

- I have to come up with two works of literature that I know well and that support or refute this quotation.

- I have to write a one-sentence conclusion.

Most critical lens quotations have a semantic component: the student has to explain what we mean by a certain word or phrase. In this one, the student has to define (interpret) "frozen sea within us." This metaphor can be interpreted as a vast part of us that is unaware (frozen), whether intellectually or emotionally. Here are some other examples of critical lens quotations with semantic implications:

- "In literature, evil often triumphs, but never conquers." What do we mean by the words *triumph* and *conquer*? We have to establish a distinction in order to write the essay.

- "The fundamental things apply, as time goes by." What do we mean by *fundamental things* (other than moonlight and love songs)?

- "Literature is news that *stays* news" (Ezra Pound). What do we mean by *news*?

- "Stories, like whiskey, must be allowed to mature in the cask" (Sean O'Faolain). What does the *whiskey/cask* metaphor convey? Is the *cask* a metaphor for the book itself or for the reader's mind?

Having established what the quotation means, the student must then agree or disagree with it, as she has interpreted it. This can be done in one sentence.

Next is the criteria statement, which is what students have the most difficulty with. The question is: What does a work of literature have to do, have, or be in order to support or refute this statement? Does it have to affect the reader emotionally? Cause the reader to reflect? Does it have to show particular themes? Have interesting characters? Have a social impact? The criteria statement can be a single sentence, based on a sentence stem such as these:

- In order for a story to satisfy this quotation, it would have to _____, or

- A story that illustrates this quotation would have _____, or

- You could say that a story embodies this quotation if it _____.

Next, the writer would name the literature, using the proper conventions for punctuating the title and naming the author.

Whether the above information could be given in one or two paragraphs is a stylistic choice.

Next, the writer addresses the first work of literature, showing, by referring to (not summarizing) events that support or refute the quotation. This could take one or two paragraphs, and then a segue into the next work and a brief conclusion that refers to the quotation.

It's easy to confuse critical questions with thematic ones. The critical question requires interpretation, establishment of criteria and evaluative thinking. The thematic question is the well-known *In literature, as in life...* set-up:

> In literature, as in life, characters often have mentors. From the works of literature that you have read, choose two in which a character has a mentor and show by specific references how that mentor influences the character by words and deeds.

In this type of question, the criterion is already present; the character/mentor relationship has to be there. Also, the writer is not invited to agree or disagree with the statement, or even to interpret it.

The distinction between a critical quotation and a thematic one is not always clear. The following quotations call for critical thinking because they are open to interpretation.

- ♦ "A good book makes the world harder to understand."

- ♦ "Life is what happens while you're busy making other plans." —John Lennon

- ♦ "The most disturbing horror in a story is horror that takes place in the midst of ordinary life, commonplace activities, or pleasant surroundings."—Alan Porter

- ♦ "The setting is like another character in the story. The setting skulks in, cold, brooking and sinister; it dances into music on warm summer nights, all glittering and whispering; or the setting hangs over the story oppressively like a layer of dust."

- ♦ "The most perceptive writers portray the irony of human behavior; how one's sense of duty and responsibility leads to tragedy or sorrow; how human hands are capable or evil deeds; how human hopes and dreams are manufactured from illusions."

- ♦ "Readers are most affected by writers who end their stories with a character's positive moral development. Even if the character is at the point of death, he or she comes to terms with what he or she feels is right and good."

STANDARDS

The critical lens essay meets the Standards because students have to interpret, analyze, and evaluate the quotation and the literature. They have to write an essay using the conventions of formal standard written English.

CHALLENGE LEVEL

The challenge is to approach the task in an organized way: First, to interpret the quotation and its semantic ambiguities; second, to agree or disagree; third, to establish criteria; and finally, to discuss the literature accordingly.

MULTIPLE INTELLIGENCES

Students who learn best by using a spatial/visual schemata should make a map of the components of the critical lens essay.

SCORING GUIDE

- ◆ Meaning: You've interpreted the quotation, agreed or disagreed, established criteria, and discussed the literature accordingly.

    4. _____

    3. _____

    2. _____

    1. _____

- ◆ Development: You've done a thorough job of referring to the specifics of the literature and how they relate to the quotation.

    4. _____

    3. _____

    2. _____

    1. _____

- ◆ Organization: You've followed the appropriate organizational pattern for an essay, including topic sentences, paragraph structure, transition, introduction and conclusion.

    4. _____

    3. _____

    2. _____

    1. _____

- ◆ Word Choice: Your vocabulary and sentence structure are interesting, varied, and appropriate for a literary essay.

    4. _____

3. _____

2. _____

1. _____

♦ Presentation: You've observed the conventions of formal standard written English in spelling, capitalization, sentence structure, and punctuation.

4. _____

3. _____

2. _____

1. _____

FOLLOW-UP

The literary essay based on the critical lens can vary in length and can require any number of works in a variety of genres.

SAMPLES OF STUDENT WORK

ASHTON: HIGH LEVEL

"A good book should serve as the ax for the frozen sea within us."
—Franz Kafka

When an ax breaks up ice, the water is able to flow. To the mind, the flow is thinking and feeling emotions. This is what I think Franz Kafka is saying about what a book can do. I agree with this quotation because I've read books that had ideas that flowed in my mind. A book that breaks up the frozen sea within us would have to have characters and situations that get you involved in an emotional way. They awaken compassion in you, or even make you want to cry. Two books that had this effect on me are The Poisonwood Bible by Barbara Kingsolver and Angela's Ashes by Frank McCourt.

Both of these books described the death of children because of poverty. In the novel The Poisonwood Bible, Ruth May dies when she is bitten by a snake. She also had malaria and was very weak. Ruth May was the youngest of the four children. She was maybe eight or ten when she tragically dies. This family wasn't really poor but they lived like they were poor because they were living in the Congo as missionaries. In the memoir Angela's Ashes, Frank's two brothers die of diseases caused by poor living conditions and lack of medical care. Both of these books made me want to cry when the children died.

Another reason why these books were an emotional experience for me is that they are both about families where the father has a negative impact on the family because of his behavior. Frank McCourt's father was an alcoholic and you never knew what he would do when he was drunk. In The Poisonwood Bible, the father was a religious fanatic and he eventually went insane in the jungle. In both families, the father's obsessions decided what happened to the mother and children and I thought this was very sad.

So after I read these two books, I felt like something had melted inside me because I felt real emotions for what happened to the characters.

COMMENTARY

When writing about two works of literature, we have to be sure to integrate them. We can't have what amounts to two separate essays that happen to be on the same page. Ashton has done a good job of transitioning from one novel to the next, and then bringing both back together in the conclusion. Note the correct use of the terms *novel* and *memoir*. This may seem like a small point, but it signifies the student's ability to make the important distinction between fiction and nonfiction and it shows the positive learning habit of using accurate terminology. That habit will serve the student well not only in English, but across the curriculum.

COLE: MID LEVEL

"A good book should serve as the ax for the frozen sea within us."
—Franz Kafka

I think that Franz Kafka means that a good book should conquer the unknowns in your mind. The "frozen sea" is all that you don't know about life like how people live in other places, times, and with problems that you may never know. I agree with this quotation because after I've read a good book I feel that I've broken up a part of me that was frozen, that didn't know something about life. In order to satisfy this quotation, a book would have to make you understand something about life that you never thought about or didn't understand. Two novels that do this are The Poisonwood Bible by Barbara Kingsolver and Angela's Ashes by Frank McCourt.

In The Poisonwood Bible a family goes to the Congo in the early 1960s to be missionaries. The mother and four children don't want to go but the father believes in doing God's work. They find out that Africa changes them more than they change Africa and they can never be the same. When the Congo fights for independence, this family is not wanted there but the father refuses to leave and the mother and daughters feel that they have no power. They have terrible disasters such as snakebites, malaria, an "ant river" and violence.

This book serves as an ax for the frozen sea within me because it made me understand something that I've never thought about before. It made me understand how the Congo is so poor. They didn't have any of the conveniences of home and they got sick and injured. The Congo was the frozen sea for me. Now when I think of Africa I have a picture of it in my mind, not what it looks like but what it would actually be like to live there day today.

Another book that showed me what it was like to live in a different place and not have any of the conveniences that I'm used to is <u>Angela's Ashes</u> by Frank McCourt. In this book, it is about a large family that lives in Ireland in a very poor section. Many of the children die from diseases that wouldn't happen if they had good health care. My frozen sea was that I didn't know what it was like to live in Ireland and how poor it was.

Books can break up the frozen sea within us by showing us how other people live at other times and places.

COMMENTARY

Cole has a good idea of what the quotation means and how it applies to these two works, but he fails to refer to characters by name. Note the awkward constructions (In this book it is about) and the reference to *Angela's Ashes* as a book, rather than as a memoir. The premise, that the metaphor means that a good book helps you to understand something, is too broad, which is why the references are also too broad.

JARETT: LOW LEVEL

The Poisonwood Bible and Angelas Ashes are two books I read that are examples of the ax that serves the frozen sea within us.

The Posionwood Bible is about a family that goes to Congo to be missionaries. They are in for surprises. There are four daughters. Two are twins. One of the twins is half parilized but then she teaches her self how to walk. Later the father goes off into the jungle and no one ever hears *from him again. One of the girls opens up a hotel and gets rich living in Africa. The Congo got there independance.*

The other book is Angelas Ashes. The true story of an author who grew up very poor in Ireland. His brothers died of diseases. His father is a drunk and can't keep his job. There house smells like sewage.

Both of these books were good and they showed about poor people.

COMMENTARY

Jarett does not grasp what the thinking procedure should be here. He begins by misquoting Kafka and never does say what he thinks it means. Jarett is comfortable in the summary zone, and he probably doesn't know how to move off from it. The statement "They are in for surprises" misrepresents the serious tone of the novel. Note the lack of punctuation of the titles and the failure to mention authors or genres.

PROPOSING A BOOK FOR SUMMER READING

PRODUCT: A PROPOSAL

In this task, students write a proposal for a book to be assigned as summer reading.

DIRECTIONS TO THE STUDENTS

Our school has established a Summer Reading Committee and is looking for recommendations. The committee consists of teachers, administrators, parents, and students. Their mission is to put out a list of books from which students will choose two titles to read over the summer.

What book would you recommend for summer reading? Write a proposal to be presented to the Summer Reading Committee in which you give your reasons for recommending a particular title. Explain why this book would be of interest to students and why it has enough literary value to appeal to teachers. Your proposal should be one page long. The book can be a novel, collection of short stories, memoir, or biography.

INSTRUCTION

This task can come out of a *book-of-choice* unit. Students need to be familiar with a wide variety of books. The proposal should address these questions:

- Why do you think this is a good title for summer reading for your peers?

- If you know anyone else who has read this book, what do they think?

- Are there any reviews of this book on the Net? You might want to quote these.

- Why would adults approve of this book for summer reading?

- Who is the author? What else has he or she written?

- Who is the publisher? Is the book still in print?

- Is the book appropriate for high school students? Is it too easy or too challenging for students to read on their own?

In addition to these considerations, the student has to establish a purpose for summer reading. Is it supposed to be pleasure reading or academic reading? Do we eliminate any books that have *objectionable* content? What about books that have been made into movies? What about books for which commercial study guides are available? Should the book or author have name recognition?

To instruct for this task, you need to make students aware of audience needs. Who are the constituents (students, teachers, administrators, parents) and what would they need to hear about a summer reading title?

The proposal needs to be a mix of summary and enough literary criticism to justify its inclusion on the list. Students need to establish criteria and show how a given title suits them.

STANDARDS

This task meets the Standards because it requires students to show awareness of audience and to have read a wide variety of literature. To propose a book, students may have done a cursory reading of it, thus adjusting reading rate to suit the purpose.

CHALLENGE LEVEL

The challenge of this task is to appeal to a double audience (students and adults) who have divergent motivations, and to justify an opinion on literature rather than to simply say that a book is *good*.

MULTIPLE INTELLIGENCES

In addition to verbal/linguistic intelligence, this task, being a sales pitch, requires interpersonal intelligence because the students have to know what their peers and the adult audience would agree to.

SCORING GUIDE

- Meaning: Your proposal includes all of the elements required in the task description.

    4. _____

    3. _____

    2. _____

    1. _____

- Development: You've provided adequate information about the book and support for your recommendation.

    4. _____

    3. _____

    2. _____

    1. _____

- Organization: You've presented your ideas in a logical order with transition.

    4. _____

    3. _____

    2. _____

    1. _____

- Word Choice: Your vocabulary and sentence structure are varied, interesting, and appropriate.

    4. _____

    3. _____

    2. _____

    1. _____

♦ Presentation: You've observed the conventions of spelling, capitalization, punctuation, and sentence structure and you've used the proper conventions for referring to a book.

4. _____

3. _____

2. _____

1. _____

FOLLOW-UP

Your school might actually like to enact a Summer Reading Committee that would review these proposals and make recommendations. Students would have to do whatever writing would be required to form such a committee: draft a mission statement, make announcements to recruit members, and then make an annotated list of recommended reading.

SAMPLES OF STUDENT WORK

ALAINE: HIGH LEVEL

We All Fall Down by Robert Cormier. Bantam Doubleday

I'm not usually a reader, in fact reading is about the last thing I would ever want to do in the summer, but I have to admit that I couldn't put this book down and I even read two more books by this author, Tenderness and The Bumblebee Flies Anyway. My friend Brian recommended this book to me when I saw him reading it at work when we were on our break. Like me, Brian doesn't usually read in his spare time.

The book start out describing a trashing of a house. It turns out that one of the trashers is a kid named Buddy Walker. He ends up falling in love with Jane Jerome, whose house he trashed, not knowing it was her, and she doesn't know he was one of the trashers. The story is also about the Avenger, a deranged neighbor who witnessed the trashing.

The review on Amazon.com says: "The author expertly twists both plot and characters in this shocking study of the effects of random violence." This book would appeal to both boys and girls who like books that are about teenagers and have a dark side. It does have some objectionable language in the beginning but it's really about the story and not the language. It also has some good words in it that we had in our vocab notes and some words I didn't know. I didn't look them up.

I recommend this book for summer reading because it isn't the usual type of book you read in school and I think it might get some kids to start reading other books

COMMENTARY

Alaine meets the requirements of the task by referring to other books by this author, another reader and a review. She considers that his peers would like the book because it has a dark side, and that adults would approve because it might inspire other reading. Alaine does mention the objectionable language, and that it is appropriate to the nature of the story. (Her comments on vocabulary are expressed in an immature way, but the intention is endearing.)

TJ: MID LEVEL

I recommend the novel <u>The Great Santini</u> by Pat Conroy. This book is about a family that is dominated by a father who calls himself The Great Santini. The father's real name is Bull Meecham. He is a marine fighter pilot and he runs the family like a military dictatorship. The story centers around the oldest son Ben. Ben will never please his father, no matter how good an athlete he is. Ben is trying to protect his mother and sister from his father's violence. He is trying to understand why his mother stays with his father, who is so violent.

I think kids would like this book because it has a lot of action and interesting characters that take place in school. Also if you are interested in basketball you would like it.

COMMENTARY

We get a feel for the book here but the audience shifts to the second person for no reason. Note the lack of reference to reviews, to other readers, and to other books by this author.

MAUREEN: LOW LEVEL

The book I recommend for summer reading to the summer reading committee is called Athletic Shorts by Chris Crutcher. These are stories that are about sports. Some of the sports are basketball, football, and wrestling. Common issues and themes in young-adult literature are explored from an unconventional perspective in these short stories featuring, for the most part, characters readers will recognize from Crutcher's popular novels. The dialogue is quick and scorching, and the character-

izations are powerfully drawn. Crutcher is a discerning reporter of the in-ner life of adolescent males. In these storys they are always about a teen-age kid who has problems.

COMMENTARY

Note the obvious verbatim copying from a review.

REMEDIATION

The following questions will help students focus on features of the book that would justify their recommendation:

- ◆ For your peers:
  - Does the story have suspense?
  - Does the story remind you of people you know?
  - Are there surprises in the story?
  - Would the story make a good movie?
- ◆ For your teachers:
  - Would the story make kids want to read another story like this one?
  - Is the story like anything else we've read in class?
  - Does the story have new words or words that we've learned?

SUMMARY

The tasks in this chapter teach students how to apply elementary principles of literary criticism. These are high-level thinking tasks because they involve the establishment of criteria and the evaluation of literary traits against them. Students at the high school level are ready to move beyond the literal level when speaking about literature, but they need much guidance and practice to do so. The tasks shown here invite students to consider what the qualities of good literature are for a given purpose and then justify their assertions using lit-erary language.

10

PERFORMANCE TASKS BASED ON FULL-LENGTH WORKS

CHAPTER OVERVIEW

Full-length works—novels, plays, biographies, movies, and memoirs—are the mainstay of the high school English curriculum. What we have students do with full-length works determines how well they understand, remember, and appreciate literature and how well they apply it to their own lives.

Most novels, plays, biographies, movies and memoirs were intended as entertainment, not as fodder for homework, projects, and tests. Recall Mark Twain's notice to the readers of *The Adventures of Huckleberry Finn:*

> Persons attempting to find a motive in this narrative will be prosecuted; persons attempting to find a moral in it will be banished; persons attempting to find a plot in it will be shot.—By order of the author.

Although Twain's tongue-in-cheek warning signals the ironic tone of the whole tale, his caveat is not without some merit: We can, indeed, destroy the joy of literature by reducing it to an academic exercise.

That said, what is the purpose of the performance task based on a full-length work? One purpose is assessment, of course, but a larger purpose is that the performance task should *help the reader make meaning from text.*

Plenty of pedagogical controversies buzz around the literary canon. Should we assign required reading to a whole class, or should students read books of their choice? If we give them required reading, do they all have to be at the same page at the same time, or do we just tell them to finish the whole book by a certain date? If we give them books of choice, do we limit their choices? How do we know that they are not *reading* the same book year after year? How do we know they haven't just seen the movie? Read the Cliff or Monarch notes? Pulled a paper off the Internet? Hired or cajoled someone else to write the paper? Should they be reading classics or contemporary literature? What constitutes a classic? Should they be reading popular fiction? Best-sellers? Potboilers?

The only qualification that these performance tasks demand is that the literature be rich enough to sustain serious thought, analysis, and interpretation. In other words, that they be worth the student's time. Books that are the literary equivalent of the maxim *buy cheap, get cheap*, will leave the student stymied. But literature that summons our concentration and imagination will be illuminated by these tasks:

- Writing a Thematic Paper Based on a Full-Length Work
- Reader Response Journals

WRITING A THEMATIC PAPER BASED ON A FULL LENGTH WORK

PRODUCT: LITERARY ESSAY

In this task, students write a multiparagraph essay showing how one or more full-length works use literary elements to convey a theme.

DIRECTIONS TO THE STUDENTS

Write a multiparagraph essay in which you show how two full-length works convey a theme. State your theme in the form of a thesis statement. Develop your essay by making specific references to the literature without lapsing into summary. Refer to literary elements such as *plot development, suspense, rising action, climax, denouement, character, relationships, setting, irony, symbolism, tone, structure, point of view, foreshadowing, allusion, genre, figurative language, style, contrast, motif, imagery, turning point,* and so on.

INSTRUCTION

The literary essay is the flagship of the English Language Arts curriculum. By learning the skills called upon to write the literary essay, students learn how to:

- Organize an essay around a clear thesis statement
- See beyond the literal level
- Make connections, draw conclusions, support assertions, compare and contrast
- Use literary terminology

THE FOUNDATION

In a thematic essay, the student has to come up with the theme that they express at the close of the first paragraph as *a thesis statement*. The ability to write a thesis statement is at the heart of composing an essay. (You could say that the ability to compose a thesis statement is at the heart of thinking through an idea and expressing what you know about it) Some questions make the job easy by laying out the thesis at the outset, like this:

> In literature, as in life, characters reach a point of no return. From the literature you have read, choose two works in which a character reaches a point of no return. Show by specific references how that character reaches the point of no return, why there is no return, and the circumstances leading up to and following this point. Give titles and authors.

This format does the hard part by pointing up exactly what the thesis should state. A more challenging, and therefore more meaningful, question is to approach the essay the other way around: Begin with the literature (or offer an open-ended choice of literature) and ask the students to find a common theme.

Suppose your students have read the following literature:

- *The Adventures of Huckleberry Finn* by Mark Twain

- *To Kill a Mockingbird* by Harper Lee

- *The Great Gatsby* by F. Scott Fitzgerald

- *The Scarlet Letter* by Nathaniel Hawthorne

- *Beloved* by Toni Morrison

- *Julius Caesar* by William Shakespeare

- *The Hobbit* by J.R.R.Tolkein

- *The Grapes of Wrath* by John Steinbeck

- *Tuesdays With Morrie* by Mitch Albom

- *An American Childhood* by Annie Dillard

Now the student's job is to derive a theme from any two of these works. She must then compose a thesis statement. (Note the etymological sisterhood between the Greek words *thesis* and *theme*, both denoting *to set down*.) Here's what you can tell students about how to go about the task:

HOW TO DERIVE A THEME

To derive a theme, ask yourself what the works of literature have in common. Or, ask yourself what you found interesting in *one* work. Then, see if that point of interest is present in any other work. Or, ask yourself a question that the literature evoked for you. If you find an answer to that question, that answer may be your theme, if you can also find the same answer in another work. Or, you can settle upon something you happen to be interested in, and see if the literature plays into that interest.

SAMPLES OF STUDENT WORK

MITCHELL

Mitchell really liked *The Hobbit* and *The Grapes of Wrath*. These are the books that he feels he knows the most about. What do they have in common? Here is Mitchell's thesis statement.

> In John Steinbeck's <u>The Grapes of Wrath</u> and in J.R.R. Tolkein's <u>The Hobbit</u>, the main characters struggle along the path to the Promised Land, and when they finally arrive, they find that unexpected challenges await them.

SCOTT

Scott was interested in the theme of deciding what's right and wrong in *Huck Finn*. Looking over the other titles, he realized that he could bring *Julius Caesar* into this theme very easily.

> Characters question what is right and what is wrong in <u>The Adventures of Huckleberry Finn</u> by Mark Twain and <u>Julius Caesar</u> by William Shakespeare.

JAMIE

Jamie couldn't understand why Hester Prynne didn't just leave Boston when she was made to live as a pariah. When she realized that Hester stayed because she believed in bearing her misfortune and staying near the man she loved, even though he was distant from her, she saw how that theme could be applied to *Tuesdays With Morrie*.

> <u>The Scarlet Letter</u> (Nathaniel Hawthorne) and <u>Tuesdays With Morrie</u> (Mitch Albom) deal with the theme of forebearance, which means withstanding misfortune with dignity.

MEREDITH

Meredith is interested in sports. None of these titles are specifically about sports, but they are about the elements of sports: competition, mental attitude, teamwork, pushing oneself, being physically fit, learning from a coach, facing defeat, training, and dedication.

Both Annie Dillard (<u>An American Childhood</u>) and F. Scott Fitzgerald (<u>The Great Gatsby</u>) write about people who focus everything on their goal and know how to achieve it.

How to Compose a Thesis Statement

A thesis statement is an informed conclusion based on analysis of an issue. What is the thesis statement supposed to do? It is supposed to enable you to interpret the work. If the only thing it enables you to do is to retell the story, then it doesn't do enough. If you think we can encompass every single episode of a story, then your thesis statement is too broad. It has to focus on one important aspect and has to be buttressed by literary elements.

Here's the test of a good thesis statement: It evokes thought. By thought, we mean:

- Interpretation: Aside from the obvious, what is in this picture?

- Analysis: What are the parts of the picture? How do the parts come together to make the whole?

- Comparison/contrast: What is the same in both pictures? What is different?

- Reflection: How does the picture change the more we think about it?

A good thesis statement generates plenty of examples from both works. Proving a good thesis statement requires you to refer to literary elements. A weak thesis statement leads nowhere else but to a summary.

Sample of Student Work

Taylor

Taylor is struggling with his thesis statement. He wants to write about childhood.

In both <u>An American Childhood</u> by Annie Dillard and <u>To Kill A Mockingbird</u> by Harper Lee they are about childhood.

Taylor's problem here is the word *about*. Yes, we can use *about* in making a thematic statement, but we need to flag it as a *summary-talking word* rather than a *theme-talking word*. Taylor needs to focus his thesis statement by using an action verb.

In both *An American Childhood* by Annie Dillard and *To Kill A Mockingbird* by Harper Lee, the authors portray important memories of childhood.

From there, Taylor invites himself to think about *why* specific memories were important: Did the author/characters learn anything? Were these memories surprising? Poignant? Shocking? Scarring? Wonderful?

A thesis statement should marshal your literary resources, should give you a chance to show off what you've figured out about the stories based on what was already obvious.

Ironically enough, the thesis statement is a *conclusion*. These students have thought about a topic, thought about the literature and drawn a conclusion that brings the topic of choice together with the literature of choice. The body of the essay will support this conclusion.

By the way, nothing is wrong with directly stating the theme(s). *One theme is that...*. We can go on to form a strong statement. But, be careful of *about*, a word that often leads to plot summary:

> One theme of *Beloved* by Toni Morrison is that love is eternal, and it triumphs over all hardships.

WHAT ELSE GOES IN THE FIRST PARAGRAPH?

First of all, the conventional way to write an opening paragraph does not mean that the thesis statement goes first. Although placing the thesis statement as the first sentence is not against the law, it is just not the expected way to do things. In fact, the thesis statement is usually the *last sentence* of the opening paragraph. We sort of *run up to* the thesis statement by getting the reader in the mood. The mood-evoking part of the opening paragraph is called the *motivate*. A motivate is a general interest statement that sets the stage for the thesis statement.

We are using the motivate and the thesis statement to comprise the introductory paragraph. First impressions set the tone. After reading the first paragraph, the reader will know if she is in good hands or not. Your thesis statement shouldn't change much, because it determines the development of the paper, and not the other way around; but you may want to tweak it later.

Here are suggestions about writing the sentences that will set the stage for the thesis statement:

- Make a general statement about your topic to establish a context for your essay; *or*

- Begin with an anecdote. An anecdote is simply a brief story; *or*

- Begin with a question; *or*

♦ Do something else.

SAMPLES OF STUDENT WORK

MITCH

Life is a journey. We have destination and a map, but there are plenty of traffic jams, unmarked roads, detours, delays, roadside attractions, and highway robbers. And when we finally arrive at our destination, it isn't what we thought it would be and we don't feel the way we thought we would feel. In John Steinbeck's <u>The Grapes of Wrath and in J.R.R. Tolkein's The Hobbit, the main characters struggle along the path to the Promised Land, and when they finally arrive, they find that unexpected challenges await them.</u>

SCOTT

The most important distinction that we can make in life is the distinction between right and wrong. You'd think that you could look it up in a lawbook or the Bible, but it isn't always that easy. Sometimes, you get conflicting messages about what's right or wrong in a give situation. Then, you have to search your heart. Characters question what is right and what is wrong in <u>The Adventures of Huckleberry Finn</u> by Mark Twain and <u>Julius Caesar</u> by William Shakespeare.

JAMIE

We've all heard the expression "Don't give up." That's easy to say, but what about when you are an outcast or if you are terribly ill and there is no hope for your recovery? Some people can hold their heads up in such dire circumstances and be deserving of admiration instead of pity. <u>The Scarlet Letter</u> (Nathaniel Hawthorne) and <u>Tuesdays With Morrie</u> (Mitch Albom) deal with the theme of forbearance, which means withstanding misfortune with dignity.

MEREDITH

When you want something badly enough, you have to know how to get it and you have to set your priorities up so that you do whatever is necessary. You can't be distracted or do what is easy if you want to reach your goal. Both Annie Dillard (<u>An American Childhood</u>) and F. Scott Fitzgerald (<u>The Great Gatsby</u>) write about people who focus everything on their goal and know how to achieve it.

TAYLOR

You may not realize it at the time, but as you go about your childhood, you are taking pictures. These are not real pictures. They are mental pictures that you will always look back on later in your life in the scrapbook of your mind. In both <u>An American Childhood</u> by Annie Dillard and <u>To Kill A Mockingbird</u> by Harper Lee the authors portray important memories of childhood.

THE DEVELOPMENT

Here's what you can tell students so that they can use literary elements to develop their essay:

Your topic sentence should contain a literary word. Then, present supportive sentences that refer to each work. Then, bring the two works back together in light of the literary word that governs the paragraph.

Note how the following paragraphs lead off with a literary element, give examples from each book, and then tie both books together in a thematic statement.

SAMPLES OF STUDENT WORK

MITCH

<u>The turning point of</u> *both novels is when the traveling party finally reaches their destination. For the Joads, the Promised Land is California, where they were supposed to find plenty of work, food, and a new life full of opportunity. To their dismay, not all of their party is still alive. Not only that, but they are not welcome to the Promised Land, and they find it full of corruption and more starvation. As for Bilbo and company, when they finally arrive at the Lonely Mountain, they have to make yet another journey before they can get in the door. In both stories, the journey is going to be longer than they thought and fraught with more danger.*

SCOTT

<u>The setting</u> *of both works demands that the main characters question the laws of the land. In <u>Huck Finn</u>, the law of the land demands that Huck turn Jim in as a runaway slave, but he tears up the letter and decides to go to Hell rather than obey the law. In Julius Caesar, Brutus wrestles with his conscience to decide if the laws of a democratic Rome can be maintained*

under Caesar. In another time and place, these struggles of the heart would not be necessary the way they are here.

JAMIE

As soon as you look at Hester or Morrie, you see <u>the symbol</u> of their suffering. For Hester, this is the letter A, and for Morrie the symbol of his suffering is his wheelchair. The challenge for both Hester and Morrie is to not let their symbols dictate how they feel about themselves and their lives. A wheelchair isn't the same kind of symbol as a badge of shame, but they both represent a disability that society looks at you and knows things about you that are not their business. Both the wheelchair and the A cause great pain and many tears but Morrie and Hester know that love is more important than their symbols.

MEREDITH

A <u>recurrent motif</u> in <u>An American Childhood</u> and <u>The Great Gatsby</u> is love of the American heartland. The difference is that Annie Dillard keeps her love of nature, whereas Jay Gatsby loses his love of the American heartland and instead adopts the corrupt values of the Big City. F. Scott Fitzgerald writes beautiful passages about the Midwest, but the irony of the story is that although Jay Gatsby achieved his goal of becoming rich and loved by Daisy, he destroyed himself by falling for corrupt values. So the motif of nature has a different meaning in these works. For Annie, it stays pure, whereas for Gatsby, it loses its meaning.

TAYLOR

Both <u>An American Childhood</u> and <u>To Kill A Mockingbird</u> have <u>images</u> of collections. Many children collect things and treasure them. Annie Dillard's neighbor gives her a rock collection that she cherishes. Scout's neighbor gives her odd figures which he leaves in the hollow of a tree. Scout cherishes two carved figures of herself and Jem. In both works, the childhood collections evoke pleasant images of being part of a neighborhood.

Thus it is that "The words in the thesis and the construction of that sentence create a contract with the reader, a contract which it is your job to fulfill in the essay" (Vavra).

THE CONCLUSION

For reasons of etiquette, we write a conclusion. A conclusion gives the paper a finished edge and says a proper good-bye to the reader. Each paper is different, so there is no formula for writing a conclusion, but here are some suggestions:

- Check your brainstorming notes for an idea. You are even more likely to find something in your brainstorming notes that you did not use, which can be adapted for a conclusion. For example, if you are writing about the advantages of hunting with a bow and arrow, the conclusion might suggest a few good local places to do such hunting; *or*

- Consider your intended audience and attempt to reemphasize how the essay related to them; *or*

- Go for the macro. Show how the theme that you've been discussing applies to the larger universe; *or*

- Suggest how the thesis could be considered from different perspectives; *or*

- Appeal to Mount Olympus. A classy way to end an essay is with a classical reference. You can also refer to a legend, the Bible, Shakespeare, or other literature; *or*

- Tie the ends of the two stories together; *or*

- Say a word about the importance of this theme to you personally; *or*

- If you cannot think of anything else, summarize, but do not tell the reader that you are doing so. Concluding a three to four page paper with a summary can insult many readers. In essence, you are telling the readers that they are too stupid to remember three pages of material. If you can't think of anything else to do, then summarize, but do not use "In conclusion," or "In sum;" *or*

- Do something else.

SAMPLES OF STUDENT WORK

MITCH

At the end of Bilbo's journey, Gandalf remarks: "You are not the little hobbit that you were." Bilbo is no longer the comfortable creature that he was at the beginning of the book. Likewise, the Joad family has changed.

Some members have died, some have wandered off. In these and many other journey tales, it's the journey itself and not the destination alone, that transforms the characters.

COMMENTARY

Mitch's essay is well-organized, well-supported, and clear. That's because he chose a theme (and literature) that is easy to handle and yet enables higher-level thinking. We don't usually associate *The Hobbit* with *The Grapes of Wrath* and some of their parallels are surprising. Mitch noticed that both expeditions had 13 members, but he didn't connect this number to the 12 disciples of Christ, a connection that is beyond the reach of literary novices.

SCOTT

I was interested in this topic because I was once in a situation in which my loyalty to a friend had to be tested against my loyalty to my parents. It was a difficult situation and I still don't know if I did the right thing.

COMMENTARY

Scott has approached this task with much sincerity. Throughout the paper, he has maintained focus: the struggle of conscience in the absence of an external moral compass that the individual trusts. He has shown insight into Huck and Brutus and their societies.

JAMIE

Part of religion is to try to understand what to do when suffering visits your door. Although Hester and Morrie don't really talk what their religion means to them, they bear their suffering by having relationships with others and knowing that what they've done with their lives is right.

COMMENTARY

Although it's difficult work with two different genres, Jamie has chosen a theme, forbearance, that works for Hester and Morrie. She has done a good job of recognizing the difference between Hester's socially imposed problems and Morrie's physical ones. She has emphasized the importance of maintaining a positive mental attitude and loving relationships to withstand suffering.

MEREDITH

Whether in sports or in literature it's important to test your limits. In Greek mythology there is a story about Icarus, who tests his limits but he flies too close to the sun and melts his wings and meets his death. Annie Dillard tests her limits by dedicating herself to writing, learning, and art. She grew up to be a successful writer. Jay Gatsby was a fictional character *who tested his limits but he flew too close to the sun by falling in love with a selfish woman and doing everything to impress her.*

COMMENTARY

Meredith is stretching it here. It is difficult and awkward to compare a novel to a memoir; they differ in structure and purpose. Despite her efforts, Annie Dillard just doesn't compare well to Jay Gatsby and her theme of *doing one's best* doesn't quite work throughout the paper. Meredith loses track of her theme in a desperate attempt to draw similarities, any similarities, between the two works.

TAYLOR

You learn a lot of history by reading about the childhoods of Annie Dillard and Scout. From Annie Dillard you learn a lot about the area of Pittsburgh in the 1950s and from Scout you learn about Alabama in the Great Depression era.

COMMENTARY

Taylor loses his point of view here by shifting to the second person. A better approach would have been a brief comparison/contrast between the two works: *To Kill a Mockingbird* is a tale of dramatic events in which ordinary memories form the background; the Dillard memoir consists of a series of soft pictures that are not galvanized by any dramatic event. Taylor's essay is another reason why we caution students against mixing genres.

A NOTE ON MIXING GENRES

Even though we've made the point that mixing genres in the thematic essay is generally inadvisable, we should still offer students the option to do so. Part of the task is going through trial and error to settle upon choices that will work for us.

CONVENTIONS OF THE LITERARY ESSAY

Students should be told to observe the following conventions when preparing their essays:

♦ Couple the title with the author in the first paragraph. After that, you may mention the title without naming the author.

♦ At the first mention of a work of literature, refer to it by its proper genre: a novel, memoir, biography, and so on. Thereafter, you may refer to it as literature, a work of literature, a story, or a piece. You may refer to novels, biographies, or memoirs as *books*, but you should not refer to a play as a *book*.

♦ A full-length work of literature has many themes. Therefore, we avoid the expression *the theme* unless we are sure we are speaking of the one pervasive idea.

STANDARDS

The thematic essay addresses all of the Standards related to literary thinking. The student has to discern, and name, similarities and differences. The thematic essay trains students not only in literary thinking, but in systematic thinking in general, which can be applied to all aspects of life. Pattern finding is key to systematic thinking. The thematic essay isn't just a matter of noticing isolated symbols or an example of foreshadowing. It is a matter of finding similarities and making connections between the characters, setting, symbols, allusions, metaphors, chapter openings and closings, and so forth.

CHALLENGE LEVEL

The challenge lies in the selection of theme and literature and then in establishing a thesis statement. From there, the task gets easier *if* the thesis statement does its job of *enabling interpretation.*

MULTIPLE INTELLIGENCES

The literary essay is not a multiple intelligence task. It is a task of verbal/linguistic skill. However students can use visual/spatial skills to make outlines and graphic organizers to help them clarify their thinking.

SCORING GUIDE

♦ Meaning: You have drawn two works of literature together by showing how their literary elements express a theme. Your thesis statement enables literary interpretation.

4. _____

3. _____

2. _____

1. _____

♦ Development: You have referred to several literary elements, providing specific examples and quotations from the literature.

4. _____

3. _____

2. _____

1. _____

♦ Organization: Your first paragraph consists of a motivator and a thesis statement. Your development paragraphs are supportive of topic sentences that refer to literary elements. You have an appropriate conclusion.

4. _____

3. _____

2. _____

1. _____

♦ Word Choice: Your vocabulary is interesting, varied, and appropriate. Your sentences are varied, concise, and clear.

4. _____

3. _____

2. _____

1. _____

♦ Conventions: You have observed the rules of spelling, punctuation, capitalization, sentence structure and presentation.

4. _____

3. _____

2. _____

1. _____

FOLLOW-UP

The structure that we've learned here can be applied to other modes of discourse, such as argumentation, for writing across the curriculum.

REMEDIATION

High school students should choose a theme that is fairly easy to work with, rather than something that stretches interpretation or mixes genres. Using a literary essay map, such as that in Figure 10.1, will help students.

FIGURE 10.1. LITERARY ESSAY MAP

Opening Paragraph (Motivator sentence(s)):	
Thesis Statement	
	Use these literary words in each topic sentence of the body paragraphs:
Paragraph 2: Topic sentence, employing a literary term. Sentence(s) about Literature 1. Sentence(s) about Literature 2. Sentence that brings both works back to the topic sentence.	• plot development • suspense • rising action • climax • denouement • character trait • relationship
Paragraphs 3, 4, 5, etc. same as above	• character development • setting • irony • symbolism • tone • structure • point of view • narration • foreshadowing • allusion • genre • figurative language • style • contrast • motif • imagery • turning point
Conclusion: One or two sentences, giving the essay a finished edge.	

READER RESPONSE JOURNALS

The term *reader response journal* refers to any number of structured note-taking activities that engage the reader in text. We know that reading comprehension improves when the reader has a purpose and can use prior knowledge to integrate new knowledge. We also know that reading literary text requires different skills and a different level of attention than does reading informational text.

Unlike informational text, which is straightforward, literary text *plays with the reader.* A story may have irony, where the reader is expected to see holes in the narrator's story, and to regard the narrator with skepticism. It may raise questions about good and evil that it does not go on to answer. In showing us the vagaries of human behavior, and the way people treat each other, a work of literature may make the world harder, not easier, to understand. It may be contradictory, humorous, or deliberately evasive and coy. The story may play with the reader by withholding key parts of a mystery. Obviously, if the mystery were laid out for us in the opening pages, there would be no point in reading the rest of it. And, the story may play with the reader by other literary conventions: shifting narrators, speaking in dialect, scrambling the order of events, or leaving the reader with unanswered questions.

The reader can skip parts of informational text, but a character in a literary text could die of consumption, move to Arizona, or fall into a vat of tar in any given paragraph and we would have no way of knowing that. If we skip the descriptive parts, we cheat ourselves of that part of the literary experience that we know as *sense of place.* Without sense of place, we can't activate the movie of the mind that is literature.

In a literary text, you must expect the unexpected. In an informational text, you have cues, such as headings, subheadings, pull quotes, charts, and graphs, that tell you what to expect.

PRODUCT: DOUBLE-ENTRY READER RESPONSE JOURNAL

In this task, students participate in the text by showing what they understand and don't understand as they go along.

DIRECTIONS TO THE STUDENTS

In a double-entry journal, the reader keeps track of the literal level of the story on the left side, and various forms of response on the right. The left (literal) side can consist of quotations or notes on story events. The response (right) side can include:

- Sensory details

- Historical background

- Predictions

- Contradictions

- Reminders

- Evocations

- Summaries

- Points of confusion

- New words

- Interesting phrases

- Coincidences

- Key verbs

Your right side notes should be twice as long as your left side notes. Plan to have approximately *one* page of notes for every *ten* pages of text.

INSTRUCTION

Reading fine literature is an acquired taste for most people who either don't read at all, or don't read with much patience. To develop the quality of patience in your readers, explain to them that there are certain agreements that the reader and the author have. We are calling this agreement *the literary contract*.

THE LITERARY CONTRACT

What we mean by *the literary contract* is that the reader and the author make certain promises to each other.

The reader promises to…

- Give the book at least 50 pages before giving up.

- Read with a serious attitude in a well-lit and quiet place, when I am not tired.

- Not skip anything

- Picture the pictures, hear the sound, feel the textures in my mind.

- Reread confusing parts.

The author promises to:

- Surprise the reader at various points.
- Tie in all elements of the story.
- Respect the reader's intelligence.
- Not write anything worth skipping.
- Write pictures you can picture, sounds you can hear, and textures you can feel.

The teacher promises to:

- Give you enough time to read
- Answer your (informed) questions
- Tell you the historical background that you need
- Share her enthusiasm for the book
- Reward your efforts

SCORING GUIDE

- Your reader response journal is:

  Complete _____

  Incomplete _____

  Insufficient _____

- Your responses indicate:

  Careful and thoughtful reading _____

  Inconsistent care and thought in reading _____

  Superficial reading _____

- The appearance of your journal can be described as:

  Neat and legible _____

  Inconsistently neat and legible _____

  Not neat and not legible _____

SAMPLES OF STUDENT WORK

TREVOR: HIGH LEVEL: THE COUNT OF MONTE CRISTO

Literal	Response
Chapter 13: Dantes looks at himself in the mirror; hadn't seen himself in 14 years "his eyes wore a look of deep sadness" 33 years olds	Will Dantes get his wealth on the Isle of Monte Cristo?
	Remember: the ship full of Turkish carpets and riches; is it ominous??
Chapter 14: they finally land at the I of MC	something bad has to happen; can't be this easy
Dantes takes a gun; finds the caves	someone will recognize him
finds the precious stones	atmosphere: tense, suspenseful
goes ashore with English passport	luck: plays big part in story
	reminds me of Les Mis: falsely accused; serves time; is free; gets rich??
	dungeons and caves: sees in the dark treasures/ stolen & recovered loot

COMMENTARY

Trevor's responses will prove helpful to him because he's noting story features that portend later events; he has a good sense of atmosphere and makes the connection between this and Les Mis.

CLUSTERING AND CATEGORIZING

Another method of reader response is to have students cluster and categorize various elements at certain intervals. Here's how it works: At intervals in the story (every quarter-way through), readers assign a subtitle that embraces the story so far. They then make several categories such as:

- ◆ Characters: good guys/bad guys

- ◆ Places: what happens where

- ◆ Props: hand-held items, who holds them, and what's their significance in the story

- ◆ Decisions: what characters have decided what things

- ◆ Lessons learned: what characters have already learned what things

- ◆ Mother Nature: how has the weather affected the story so far?

- ◆ Times of day and night: what happens when

The cluster/categorize technique is a way to stop and reconnoiter and to give students who have not become invested in the reading a chance to understand the story up to now. As the class goes over the clusters and categories, nonreaders will pick up the story. In a perfect world, everyone would keep up with the reading. This not being so, we can hope that *late bloomers* can still catch on.

CHAPTER-KEEPERS

The *chapter-keeper* shown in Figure 10.2 is another form of reader response. The students write a one-sentence summary, one or two brief questions/observations, a memorable quotation, a memorable description, a new word (context and definition) and a headline that encapsulates the chapter.

FIGURE 10.2. CHAPTER-KEEPER

Title: *The Count of Monte Cristo*
    Chapter 13

Summary	My Questions and Observations
Dantes escapes from his ball and chain and swims to the rocks. The captain of a smuggler's boat takes him on board. They plan to unload their illegal cargo on the French coast (Monte Cristo)	Will Dantes be pursued by the guys who threw him overboard? How long until he is discovered as a fugitive in Monte Cristo?
A Memorable Quote	**A Memorable Description**
"When they reached Leghorn, Dantess was eager to see whether he would recognize himself for he had not seen his own face in fourteen years."	The ship was laden with Turkish carpets, cashmere and cloth from the Levant.
A New Word	**Headline**
piaster — a unit of currency	DANTES ESCAPES — JOINS SMUGGLERS — HEADS FOR MONTE CRISTO

REMEDIATION

The double-entry journal, the cluster/categorize technique, and the chapter-keeper are three models of reader response. Others are flow charts and story maps, annotated character lists, connect-the-dots diagrams that show relationships among characters, places, and events, and color-coded highlighting.

If we think of learning as being built on prior knowledge, perhaps we can take a kinder view of commercial study guides, movies, large print, illustrated versions of classics, audiotapes, abridgments and retellings. Many students who would give up on a *classic* can derive the essence of the story from these sources. From there, they can transfer to the unabridged text. Just as we understand the importance of introducing complex information in stages, layering new knowledge on top of prior knowledge, we should think of alternative ways of introducing complex literature.

SUMMARY

In most English classes today, the bulk of the time is spent reading novels, plays, and biographies. Well-constructed performance tasks help students understand and remember complex text *as they are reading*. The tasks shown here are appropriate for assigned reading as well as for books of choice.

11

PERFORMANCE TASKS BASED ON SHAKESPEARE

CHAPTER OVERVIEW

The performance tasks based on Shakespeare are divided into four categories:

♦ Performance: Warm-ups and skits

♦ Production: The physical aspects of the play

♦ Close Reading: Understanding the language and characters

♦ Portfolio: A comprehensive reader response

WARMING UP TO SHAKESPEARE

Many students approach Shakespeare with fear and trembling, not to mention dread and loathing. Because they think it will be boring. Why? Because they think they won't understand it. True, there will be parts of it that they won't understand, parts of it that you don't understand either.

Usually, the parts that we don't understand are the nouns—the *bare bodkin*, for example—and that's because we don't have those nouns in our society. But once someone just tells us that a bare bodkin is an unsheathed knife, then we easily see what Hamlet is talking about. So you might want to comb through some of the nouns and tell students what these things are.

The second intimidating feature of the language is the archaic use of *thee*, *thy*, *thine*, *and thou* to denote *you*. For some reason, this is very scary. Just pick out a few lines that have these weird pronouns and, for practice only, say *you* or *your* instead, just to get the meaning. Same for the Elizabethan word endings in *hath*, *doth*, *maketh*, etc. Confront these menacing words right away and deflate their power to intimidate.

These warm-ups get students to scout through the plays hunting for particular words or accessible scenes. Doing this, they get their Shakespearean feet wet. Lines that they and their classmates perform will then be old friends when they appear in context later. So, we don't necessarily have to start with Act I, Scene I. By doing it this way, we build the scaffold on which to build an understanding of the play as a whole.

Keeping in mind that *plays are for the stage, not the page,* the tasks that follow will get students on their feet: to suit the action to the word, the word to the action. These tasks are based on *Julius Caesar* and *Romeo and Juliet* but they could be used for any of the plays.

WHAT'S IN A NAME?

To prepare, the students divide themselves up into acting companies and give themselves a name based on a phrase from the play.

- *Julius Caesar* companies:
  - Dogs of War
  - The Conspiracy
  - Cry Havoc!
  - Friends, Romans, Countrymen
  - Honorable Men
- *Romeo and Juliet* companies:
  - Moonshine and Madness
  - Star-Crossed Lovers
  - Love's Light Wings
  - Braggarts, Rogues, and Villains
  - Pennyworth Players

WARM-UP ONE: TABLEAU VIVANT

THE SET-UP

Actors select a word that is repeated several times in different contexts throughout the play. They choose one line for each player and write the lines on index cards.

THE PERFORMANCE

The idea is for each actor in the company to deliver his or her line as dramatically and ceremoniously as possible. The focus is to feature the word, not its context in the play, so the lines don't have to be delivered in the order that they appear in the play.

Each actor steps forward, delivers his or her line from memory, and then strikes the appropriate pose and holds it in tableau while the next actor does the same. Thus, the company forms a *word opera* illustrating the many aspects of the starring word. For a *grand finale*, the company can say the word in unison.

INSTRUCTION

The tableau vivant (living picture) is a chance to show the flexibility of a word and how its' meaning changes with context. It is also a chance to show the poetic qualities in the sound and sense of a word, how its rhythm, as well as its meaning, places it like a gem in a setting. You might want to show students how the Shakespearean *concordance* works. This is a compendium of (almost) every word that Shakespeare ever used in the plays and sonnets, categorized alphabetically, listing all of the lines containing any given word.

FOLLOW-UP: CHARACTER OPERA

This works the same as word opera, but with a character. One actor plays the character, let's say it's Brutus, delivering a line in which he is speaking about himself; another says a line that is about Brutus and said directly to him in his presence; then, a third actor says a line about Brutus that is spoken in Brutus' absence. Select lines that display a variety of perceptions that other characters have about the featured character.

WARM-UP TWO: BRIEF SCENE INTERPRETATION

THE SET-UP

In this warm-up, the company will portray the same brief scene (not more than three or four lines) with at least three different interpretations.

Brutus: The games are done and Caesar is returning.

Cassius: As they pass by, pluck Casca by the sleeve

And he will (after his sour fashion) tell you

What hath proceeded worthy note today.

Brutus: I will do so. But look you, Cassius,

The angry spot doth grow on Caesar's brow

And all the rest look like a chidden train.

Disregard the context of this brief exchange for the moment, since students won't know anything about the play at this point. Just considering the words alone, how can we play this scene?

- Brutus and Cassius think the situation is hilarious.

- Brutus and Cassius think the situation is ominous for them.

- Brutus and Cassius think the situation is ominous for Caesar.

- Brutus and Cassius think this is an opportunity to do evil.

- Brutus and Cassius think this is entirely unimportant.

- Brutus and Cassius are two dumb guys.

- Brutus and Cassius are unaware that a gigantic earthquake has just occurred.

- Brutus and Cassius just met.

- Brutus and Cassius hate each other.

- Brutus is five years old and Cassius is his father.

- Cassius is five years old and Brutus is his father.

- Brutus has a guilty secret that Cassius doesn't know about.

- Cassius has a guilty secret that Brutus doesn't know about.

- Brutus and Cassius share a guilty secret and fear being discovered.

INSTRUCTION

Students should learn how the following tools of the actor work to alter, control, and convey meaning.

- Volume

    Actors learn that nothing speaks more loudly than a whisper. Loud or soft volume can convey fear, command, focus, control or lack of control. Volume can be used to emphasize a particular word or a whole speech. Experiment with volume control

- Pauses

    As the saying goes, timing is everything. A pause can steal the scene, portray villainy, or evoke laughter. Actors pause to emphasize, to show internal response, and to create suspense. Experiment with pauses.

♦ Gesture, facial expression, and posture

The pause gives the actor the opportunity to express meaning physically. We can see the movie actor's face in close-up, but the stage actor's body is always viewed in full, making every part of his or her physical self an instrument of meaning. Experiment with gesture, facial expression, and posture.

♦ Modulation

Meaning changes as the actor modulates his or her pitch. Pitch can show emphasis, betray lack of certainty, raise questions, or imply the way the character feels about the words. Experiment with modulation.

♦ Proximity and eye contact

A character's relationship to others and what she feels about her words can be revealed in the physical distance between one character and the others. Is she, literally, looking down her nose at others? Meeting them head on? Looking with downcast eyes? Experiment with proximity and eye contact.

♦ Stretchers and twitchers

Some words stretch out, others twitch up. When we say words such as *roar, true, lost, all, drowned,* and *villainy* we can drag them out for great dramatic effect. But when we say words like *remorseless, lecherous, treacherous,* and *kindless* we tighten our lips and practically spit them out. Experiment with stretchers and twitchers.

♦ Rumination

Many of Shakespeare's lines are said by characters who are ruminating about the words as they say them. They're not sure that what is coming out of their mouths is even true, and they seem to examine the words as if they were counterfeit bills. Look for moments in soliloquies when characters are wondering what to think. Experiment with rumination.

♦ Use of props

Try the Brutus/Cassius conversation with one or both characters holding a newspaper, a flashlight, a cell phone, or a banana. How would they handle the prop in each of the situations? Experiment with props.

◆ Reaction

Acting is reacting. Remind student actors that they aren't just wait-
ing to say their lines. They need to listen with face and body and respond to what's said. One way to practice response is to insert surprise words and lines so that the scene becomes partially improvisa-
tional. Practice with reaction.

◆ Use your space

All the stage is a world. So wander, pace, stride, stalk, stroll, amble,
saunter, swagger. Use the full length of your arms to express yourself. Look around at the space as if it is a real realm. Experiment with
your space.

All of these tools of the actor's trade work together with the words to create
meaning.

WARM-UP THREE: VOICE OF NIGHTMARE/VOICE OF LULLABY

All Shakespearean plays (all plays) have moments of fearful tension and
moments of tender comfort. For this warm-up, ask students to comb through
the play looking for a harsh speech and a soft one.

Practice reading each speech for its intended purpose, and then do the reverse, reading the harsh speech in a soft voice and vice versa.

STILL WARMING UP: BEFORE STARTING THE PLAY

How much of the meaning is dictated by the words, and how much is open
to interpretation? Shakespeare offers few stage directions. The directions lie in
the lines themselves. When Banquo observes, "My noble partner doth seem
rapt withal," the actor playing Macbeth had better looked rapt, not to mention
noble. Look for lines that direct other actors to appear certain ways. For example, Cassius has to look lean and hungry, Juliet has to be laying her cheek upon
her hand, Brutus has to look as though he's with himself at war, Romeo has to
look forlorn and lovesick for Rosalind.

PLAYS WITHIN THE PLAYS

The skits suggested below have the famous Shakespearean play-within-the
play structure, wherein your class is playing out what it would be like to perform the play.

SKIT 1: SPEAK THE SPEECH AS I PRONOUNCE IT

As you read the play and the class becomes accustomed to the action, play out a humorous skit in which a long-suffering director is valiantly trying to work with an actor who *doesn't* look the way the lines dictate. Have the director show him what the lines instruct him to do.

SKIT 2: THE UNKINDEST CUT

♦ Dramatic argument

Stage an argument between the actor playing Mercutio and the actor playing Romeo. The director has decreed that one hundred words must be deleted from the play. Romeo has suggested decimating Mercutio's Queen Mab speech, and Mercutio offers reasons why Romeo's death speech is a little on the wordy side.

SCORING GUIDE

In addition to the kinds of performances described above, you may want students to enact scenes and soliloquies. Here is a scoring guide for rehearsed performances. It assumes that class time is used for rehearsal and that students are expected to work as a company.

♦ Performance Scoring Guide

The following items are each worth 10 points, except for the first two, which are worth 20 points:

1. Memorization and preparation of lines on schedule

2. Serious and constructive attitude displayed during rehearsals.

3. Imagination and resourcefulness in obtaining and using props and costumes.

4. Effectiveness of blocking

5. Deliverance of lines: clarity, expression, understanding

6. Staying in character during performance.

7. Displaying professional comportment offstage as well as onstage.

8. Displaying energy and enthusiasm during rehearsals and performance.

Extra points: Showing leadership, initiative, problem-solving skills

PRODUCTION

TASK 1: PROBLEM-SOLVING

Directors, producers and designers have to work within a budget and various physical restraints to solve problems and create illusions. Shakespearean plays are often staged with minimal scenery and few special effects. Dramatic atmosphere is created by the words alone, by some simple props or by symbols, costuming, and theatrical conventions.

PRODUCT: A PRESENTATION WITH VISUALS

In this task, students show how they would solve a staging problem under various circumstances. They use a visual design or map.

DIRECTIONS TO THE STUDENTS

Turn your acting company into a production company and have a meeting in which you consider ways to design and stage the following points of the play. Assume that you have a small budget, no curtain, and audience on three sides.

- Stage combat, including hand-to-hand and battle scenes
- Death scenes and removing dead bodies from the stage
- Storms
- Crowd scenes
- Ghosts and visions
- Indicating various settings in the play

Present your plans to the class. Use visuals, such as drawings and maps.

INSTRUCTION

This interdisciplinary project requires inventive thinking about theatrical conventions: What will an audience accept on stage? An audience will accept a stage crew dressed in black, coming on stage with a sheath, covering up a supine actor, and escorting him offstage as a *dead man*. They will never accept the same actor simply getting up and walking off without any ritual.

An audience will accept a slow motion *fight* but they will not accept an obviously faked punch that passes itself off as real. They will accept an actor playing more than one role, but not if he comes out and announces, "I'm the apothecary now. Before, I was Tybalt." So, the first concept to be taught is that of the nature of theatrical convention.

Next, students need to see how much of the *scenery* in Shakespeare is painted in words. How do the words delimit the scenery, props, and costumes? Many plays have a key prop, usually a letter, a ring, or an article of clothing that drives the action.

How can inexpensive materials, such as fabric, be used for several scenes? One of the most appealing aspects of theater is the use of a simple prop that takes on a different meaning from scene to scene, so that the audience uses its imagination to imbue that prop with reality.

Students have to consider the nature of *visual symbolism, motifs, color,* and *music.* The design can't be a hodgepodge of whatever is practical. It must have a strong voice of its own that supports the atmosphere that the words convey.

STANDARDS

This task meets the Standards because it requires students to use both visual and textual language to interpret and express an idea. The task is literary because it requires symbolism.

CHALLENGE LEVEL

Regarding language, the challenge is to communicate a visual idea into words. There are four parts to visualization: calling forth the image, holding that image steady in the mind's eye, manipulating the image, and then imagining the image in a changed state. Thus, it is difficult to put a mental image into words while others are doing the same. How do we know that we're talking about the same thing? The interplay between the imagination and the spoken word poses a challenge.

MULTIPLE INTELLIGENCE

This task requires mathematical, spatial, musical, interpersonal, and linguistic intelligence.

SCORING GUIDE

- ◆ Design:
  - _____ is practical and within the budget.
  - _____ conveys the meaning of the scene.
  - _____ is unified with the other design elements, colors, textures.
  - _____ is inventive, original, creative, imaginative.

- ◆ Presentation:
  - • _____ is clear and well-organized.
  - • _____ is thorough.
  - • _____ has good visuals.
- ◆ Process:
  - • _____ the company worked cooperatively and respectfully with each other.
  - • _____ many ideas were considered.

TASK 2: PROPS LIST

PRODUCT: AN ANNOTATED PROPS LIST

In this task, students write an annotated list of props that would be necessary for one act (or for the entire play).

DIRECTIONS TO THE STUDENTS

Make an annotated props list for Act One. For each prop, tell that character or characters that would use it and what it is used for.

INSTRUCTION

Some stage terminology may be in order here. A prop is a hand-held item, such as a champagne glass, not to be confused with a scene piece, which is a stationary item, such as a pillar or a portrait on the wall.

Ask students to consider the function of props in a play: what are they supposed to do? What would go into a decision on whether or not to use a particular prop? If it is referred to in the lines, then we have no choice. But what about the props for a party scene? A battle? A sea scene? A love scene?

Actors like props because they give them something to do with their hands, but stage managers know that props are demanding little creatures that like to hide just before a cue. First of all, they have to be (or look) authentic for the time period. Their color has to look right, they can't be too expensive, and they might have to take a beating. Actors are nervous people: you don't want to give them glass, or anything that can spill, or cause havoc if mishandled. Anything that gets left on the stage has to be taken off in a hurry . And, speaking of leaving things on the stage, actors are notorious for carelessly leaving props on stage after they exit. Once that happens, that leftover prop, monument to a scene gone, is the star of the show. Everyone in the audience will be looking at it until someone takes it off during a scene change. So the issue takes more thought than you might think.

STANDARDS

This task meets the Standard because it requires close reading of the text and an evaluation of what physical items would amplify meaning.

CHALLENGE LEVEL

To make this task more challenging, consider how a simple item can be used symbolically: The same item can be used as a feather duster in one scene, a headdress in another, a bouquet of flowers in another. Representational use of props is an excellent exercise in creative thinking and establishes visual motifs that enhance the artistry of the production.

MULTIPLE INTELLIGENCE

This task requires visual/spatial intelligence and kinesthetic intelligence because you have to consider how objects would be used physically.

FOLLOW-UP

Have students make costume design plans. To do this they need to have a particular place and time period, and then need to research the clothing that denoted various positions in society.

SCORING GUIDE

- ◆ Your props list:
  - shows imagination _____
  - shows an understanding of the action _____
  - is practical _____
  - is complete _____
- ◆ Your props list:
  - lacks imagination _____
  - is unclear _____
  - is impractical because _____
  - is too expensive and/or hard to find _____
  - is to risky to use on stage _____
  - is incomplete _____

SAMPLE OF STUDENT WORK

HIGH LEVEL

Dogs of War: Elliot, Sam, Elaine, Diana, Mark

Props list for Act III of Julius Caesar:

Artimidorus's letter: small scroll (Artimidorus reads this and later tries to hand it to Caesar)

Conspirators: (fake) daggers to stab Caesar

Caesar: strips of red silky fabric to represent blood. Later, the conspirators will wave these around to show that they are bathing in the blood of Caesar and parading around in it.

Sharp dagger for Mark Antony to look at during "dogs of war" speech

Mark Antony reads Caesar's will: a scroll that fits inside his toga

Paper machier "stones" for crowd when they get wild at end of Act

COMMENTARY

This group has considered practicalities and has come up with the red fabric as a good solution to the *Caesar's blood* problem. Every production of *Julius Caesar* has to solve this problem, because the references to Caesar's blood on the hands of the conspirators are essential to meaning.

REMEDIATION

If students have difficulty with this task, it is probably because they haven't considered the practicalities: Do we need it? Can we get it? Can we get rid of it? Can we reuse it? If we can't use the real thing, how can we suggest the real thing? What else looks like it? If you walk through a crafts store, you will get all kinds of ideas about how inexpensive fabric-based items can be used on stage.

TASK 3: BLOCKING

PRODUCT: A WALK-THROUGH OF A SCENE

In this task, students make a plan for how they would move people about on stage.

DIRECTIONS TO THE STUDENTS

Select a scene and show how you would position and move actors on the stage. The movement of actors on stage is called blocking. Present your scene to the class as a *walk through* in which the actors read their lines. Choose one person to narrate the walk-through and to explain the reasons for the blocking.

INSTRUCTION

Decisions as to where actors are going to move on stage have to do with focus, balance, and practicalities. You don't want a character to have to push and shove through the crowd to deliver his line. Nor do you want the audience to be confused about who is speaking.

Blocking depends upon the stage space: blocking for a three-sided space or *theatre in the round* is different from what would suit a *proscenium stage*. Will the audience be elevated, or will the stage be elevated? If a play is well blocked, a photographer should be able to snap a well-balanced picture of it at any point. If not, that picture will look like a mob scene.

STANDARDS

Blocking a scene meets the Standards because it requires understanding the flow of the drama. In blocking a scene, students work with the play on a physical level, thus making it more memorable.

CHALLENGE LEVEL

Let's face it; any time students are moving around, there is a potential for chaos. Students out of their seats don't just stand there, they do something: they poke each other, get each other in head locks, hang out the window, and play with the intercom phone. So, to do blocking, you need plenty of space (such as your school's stage or chorus room) and plenty of patience.

MULTIPLE INTELLIGENCES

Blocking is a matter of working with a series of reforming geometric shapes. So, this task calls for mathematical, spatial, and kinesthetic skills.

SCORING GUIDE

- ◆ The blocking for your scene:
  - makes it easy to follow the action _____
  - is interesting and varied _____
  - uses the whole stage _____
  - moves smoothly _____
  - creates a balanced picture _____

♦ The blocking for your scene:

- is confusing _____

- is too much of the same thing _____

- uses only parts of the stage _____

- moves awkwardly _____

- does not create a balanced picture _____

CLOSE READING

CHARACTER CHART

PRODUCT: CHARACTER CHART

In this task, students complete a character chart expressing what they know about a character and how they know it.

DIRECTIONS TO THE STUDENTS

With your company, select the three characters in the play that you know the most about. For each character, come up with three character traits expressed as adjectives (Mercutio is *imaginative, humorous,* and *hot-headed*.) Be sure that the three adjectives are not synonymous. Find at least one quotation from the play that supports each trait. The quotation could be something said by the character or about the character by someone else. It can support your claim to the trait by direct or inferential means. Express this information in a chart. Give Act, Scene, and Line numbers.

INSTRUCTION

The directions for this task are self-evident, but you should encourage students to see the full range of the human condition that Shakespearean characters represent. Concentrate on contradictions, and, as you do so, point out lines that recognize contradictions within characters, such as Antony's remarks about Brutus at the end of Act V: "...and the elements/ so mixed in him that Nature might stand up/ And say to all the world, 'This was a man!'"

STANDARDS

This task requires students to analyze and interpret written and aural text, to extract salient points and to make inferences.

CHALLENGE LEVEL

Weaker students may gravitate to synonymous traits. They may say that Romeo's traits are that he's lovesick, romantic, and dreamy, all of which mean the same thing. They might not perceive his contradictions: that he is, at the same time, fickle and loyal, religious and secular, optimistic and pessimistic.

MULTIPLE INTELLIGENCES

This task calls upon interpersonal skills (perceiving contradictory character traits, inferring traits from dialogue), spatial intelligence (setting up the chart), and verbal-linguistic intelligence (reading comprehension).

SCORING GUIDE

- ◆ Meaning and Development: Your chart expresses several *different* traits of three characters and gives quotations that prove them.

    4. _____

    3. _____

    2. _____

    1. _____

- ◆ Presentation: Your chart is neat and easy to follow.

    4. _____

    3. _____

    2. _____

    1. _____

- ◆ Conventions: You've copied the quotations using the proper spelling, capitalization and punctuation. You've indicated Act, Scene, and Line numbers.

    4. _____

    3. _____

    2. _____

    1. _____

FOLLOW-UP

Students can consider traits of minor characters. They can also find ironies, such as how Julius Caesar's arrogance is the root of both his success and his destruction. The same is true of Macbeth's valor in battle, or Brutus' belief in doing honor for Rome.

SAMPLE OF STUDENT WORK

HIGH LEVEL

Character Traits Chart

Company: *The Conspiracy*
(consisting of John P., Rob M., Erin, Carissa)

Personality Trait	*Quotations*	*Situation*	*Location*
Mark Antony 1) loyal 2) insincere 3) disloyal	1) "When Caesar says 'do this' it is performed." 2) "I come to bury Caesar, not to praise him." 3) This is a slight, unmeritable man, meet to be sent on errands."	1) Antony and Caesar at the games at the beg. of play 2) Antony at Caesar's funeral; planning to do just the opposite of what he says 3) Antony says this about Lepidus just as soon he walks out of the room; means to put Lep down on the hit list	1) Act I, Sc 2, line 10 2) Act III, Sc 2, line 66 3) Act IV, Sc 1, line 11
Brutus 1) secretive 2) influential 3) trusting	1) Portia: "Make me acquainted with your cause of grief." 2) "Our course will seem too bloody, Caius Cassius, to cut the head off and hack the limb." 3) "Mark Antony, here take you Caesar's body. You shall not in your funeral speech blame us, /But speak all good you can devise of Caesar...."	1) Brutus hasn't told Portia about the conspiracy 2) Brutus tells the other conspirators not to kill Mark Antony as well as Caesar 3) Brutus trusts that Antony will not rouse the crowd against him at his funeral speech	1) Act II, Sc 1, Line 266 2) Act II, Sc 1, line 161 3) Act III, Sc 1, line 243

Personality Trait	Quotations	Situation	Location
Julius Caesar 1) perceptive 2) not perceptive 3) bossy	1) "Yond Cassius has a lean and hungry look." 2) "Et tu, Brute" 3) But I am constant as the northern star."	1) Caesar perceives some danger in Cassius 2) Caesar does not perceive any danger in Brutus 3) Caesar thinks he's the center of the universe and doesn't have to change his mind.	1) Act 1, Sc 2, line 145 2) Act 3, Sc 1, line 78 3) Act 3, Sc 1, line 60

COMMENTARY

The Conspiracy has done a creditable job in referring to an array of traits that show the complex nature of the characters. Note the omission of Cassius, who, as a villain, has few ambiguities in his nature. As such, he is *too easy.*

REMEDIATION

For some students, it might be easier to begin with the broader quotations that illustrate character, and then name the traits. They should look for lines that bear a character's name, and then ask themselves: "What does this prove about the character?"

POETIC WORD PAIRS

PRODUCT: CATEGORIZED LIST OF WORD PAIRS

In this task, students examine a Shakespearean monologue and find words that go together for various poetic reasons.

DIRECTIONS TO THE STUDENTS

In poetry, we find word pairs. We can match words for various reasons: pairs of opposites; pairs of words with the same meaning; pairs of words where one is an example of the other; words that alliterate; words that rhyme; words that *almost* rhyme. The more creative you are, the more connections and similarities you will be able to find. First, identify all the word pairs you can find; then, categorize them under headings.

INSTRUCTION

This is an opportunity to teach poetic devices. After you establish the obvious word pairs, students will come up with interesting and subtle reasons why two words in the piece go together. This exercise usually evokes the question: "Do you think Shakespeare intended for these words to go together, or did it just happen, or are we reading into it too much?" This question should lead to a discussion about the nature of creative genius, and of how, when we are good a something, we are not always aware of the details that go into it. A sports metaphor is appropriate here: Think of all the things you have to remember to swing a hockey stick. Is the hockey player aware of doing all of these things or does he just work holistically?

STANDARDS

This task speaks to comparison/contrast, poetic qualities, and understanding genre features. It also addresses the Standard that calls for multiple readings to explicate the richness of a text. And it demonstrates the organic nature of a Shakespearean speech (or any poem).

CHALLENGE LEVEL

This is an engaging and easy task. It's a good way to have students get their hands into Shakespearean language without having to worry about the whole meaning of a speech. It's remarkable how, as you do this exercise, word pairs emerge like hidden pictures.

MULTIPLE INTELLIGENCES

Verbal/linguistic and musical skills are necessary for this task because it requires the student to hear relationships in sound and rhythm.

SCORING GUIDE

+ Meaning and Development: You've found at least 10 word pairs (of various kinds) for every 20 lines of text; your word pairs are categorized under headings.

    4. _____

    3. _____

    2. _____

    1. _____

♦ Presentation and Conventions: You've copied the words correctly and your list is neat and easy to read.

4. _____

3. _____

2. _____

1. _____

FOLLOW-UP

Try the same exercise with lines, instead of words: Pair up lines from Act I and Act V. You can also pair up lines from two plays. (If you do this, you will find that the lines from a given act in one play will match the lines in the same place in another play.)

SAMPLE OF STUDENT WORK

TEXT

Romeo and Juliet
Act III, Scene 5, lines 212–225

Nurse: Faith, that it is:

Romeo is banished, and all the world to nothing

That he dares ne'er come back to challenge you;
Or if he do, it needs must be by stealth.
Then since the case so stands as now it doth,
I think it best you married with the County.
O, he's a lovely gentleman!
Romeo's a dishclout to him. An eagle, madam,
Hath not so green, o quick, so fair an eye
As Paris hath. Beshrew my very heart,
I think you are happy in this second match,
For it excels your first, or if it did not,
Your first is dead, or 'twere as good he were
As living here and you no use of him.

HIGH LEVEL

Alison, Kayla, Meggie, Jim, Lisa
Braggarts, *Rogues and Villains*

<u>Repetition</u>:
so/so
I think/I think
<u>Rhyme</u>:
dares/ne'er
'twere/were
<u>Almost Rhyme</u>:
were/here
<u>Alliteration of word endings</u>:
since/case
<u>Alliteration of word beginnings</u>:
stealth/stands
so/stands
heart/happy
here/him
<u>Words with similar meanings</u>:
nothing/ne'er
banished/dead
<u>Words with opposite meanings</u>:
living/dead
second/first
gentleman/dishclout

COMMENTARY

This group said that they found this exercise fun and that it reminded them of the game *Boggle* because what they were looking for was right in front of them but it took a while to see it.

REMEDIATION

If students have difficulty with this, give them the categories and have them locate examples.

ELIZABETHAN RHETORIC

PRODUCT: ANNOTATED EXAMPLES OF RHETORICAL TECHNIQUES

In this task, students analyze a persuasive speech in a Shakespearean play and identify key rhetorical devices.

DIRECTIONS TO THE STUDENTS

In class, we will learn about Elizabethan rhetorical devices (components and conventions of a formal persuasive speech). Your job is to find several examples of these rhetorical devices in the "Friends, Romans, Countrymen..." speech and show how these devices accomplish the orator's purpose. State the orator's purpose.

INSTRUCTION

Although Antony's funeral oration is the quintessential persuasive speech, many other speeches in Shakespeare are organized according to the five components of Elizabethan rhetoric. Learning these components of rhetoric has been a tradition of education since ancient times. Incidentally, this division is the classic way to organize an essay:

- ♦ *Exordium* (introduction): Enlists the approval of the audience; gains their attention

- ♦ *Narratio* (development): Gives the background so that the listeners fully understand the matter being discussed

- ♦ *Confirmatio* (evidence): Offers proofs, arguments, reasons, examples, references to the experts, facts and figures

- ♦ *Confutatio* (refuting the opposition): Acknowledges what the opposition might say and answers these arguments

- ♦ *Conclusio* (summing up): Summarizes and ends on a dramatic note

The divisions among these parts are more clear-cut in some speeches than in others. Other rhetorical devices are contrast; rhetorical questions; metaphor; allusions; parallel structure; refrain; and call-and-response (interplay between audience and speaker).

STANDARDS

This task meets the Standard of having students understand the features of a genre, which, in this case, is oratory. They are using literary terminology to show that they discern the purpose of the language.

CHALLENGE LEVEL

In a speech with clear-cut divisions, such as Brutus' oration, this task is not difficult. But in Antony's speech, we see that the components are recursive, and some students may find that frustrating when they go to match the speech, line by line, against their five components.

MULTIPLE INTELLIGENCES

This task is heavily reliant on verbal/linguistic skills, but it does have a mathematical/logical piece to it in terms of the five-part breakdown. Inasmuch as oratory is definitely a rhythmic mode of discourse, there is a musical quality, as well.

SCORING GUIDE

- Meaning: You've given and explained several rhetorical devices in the speech.

    4. _____

    3. _____

    2. _____

    1. _____

- Word Choice: You've used the language of rhetoric to explain what you mean.

    4. _____

    3. _____

    2. _____

    1. _____

- Presentation/Conventions: You've copied the words of the speech correctly. Your paper is neat, labeled, and easy to read.

    4. _____

    3. _____

    2. _____

    1. _____

SAMPLE OF STUDENT WORK

HIGH LEVEL

Amy, Lisa, Mindy, Scott, Sydney, Abby
Friends, Romans, Countrymen

Exordium: "Friends, Romans, Countrymen, lend me your ears./ I come to bury Caesar, not to praise him./ The evil that men do lives after them,/ The good is oft interred with their bones./ So let it be with Casear."

Antony knows that the crowd is not in favor of him because they were swayed just now by Brutus' speech. So he appeals to them (winning their approval) by saying that he isn't going to praise Caesar. Then, he gives them something to think about when he says that the good that people do is often forgotten.

Refrain: honorable man/men; that Caesar was ambitious

Antony keeps repeating these words, and every time he does he gives examples of the opposite. He gets the crowd thinking that Brutus was ambitious (not honorable) and that Caesar was honorable (not ambitious). By repeating the words, he somehow manages to switch their meaning.

Confirmatio: "He brought many captives home to Rome"/ "When that the poor had cried, Caesar had wept."/ "I thrice presented him a kingly crown which he did thrice refuse."

Antony gives many examples of how Caesar was honorable and cared for the people of Rome. That is his argument, even though he doesn't say it is his argument.

Rhetorical Question: "Did this in Caesar seem ambitious?"

Obviously, the answer is no, so Antony is asking this rhetorical question to get the crowd involved in the speech in some audience participation.

Confutatio: "But Brutus says that Caesar was ambitious/And Brutus is an honorable man"

Antony is refuting the argument that Caesar was ambitious by giving examples of how Caesar was generous.

COMMENTARY

This group, aptly named, has given a wide variety of examples and has backed up the quotations with clear explanations of how the rhetorical devices work.

REMEDIATION

Because Antony is being ironic, this might not be a good speech for weaker students to analyze. Brutus' oration is more straightforward. *Vital Speeches* is a good source for modern speeches that follow the classic techniques.

SHAKESPEARE PORTFOLIO

PRODUCT: A FORMAL COLLECTION OF WRITTEN WORK

In this task, students present various types of writing about three Shakespearean plays. This task is completed over a 12-week period.

DIRECTIONS TO THE STUDENTS

A *portfolio* is an organized collection of different types of written work. Your *Shakespeare portfolio* will contain the elements described below.

PARTS OF THE PORTFOLIO

GENERAL INFORMATION

♦ Work will be presented in a flexible three-ring binder. All pages must have reinforcements.

♦ A table of contents must be included.

♦ All sections must be marked with dividers and tabs.

LOG ENTRIES

♦ Phase One

Approximately five to seven pages, consisting of *handwritten material* that shows how your mind was working as you read the plays and learned about them in class. Your logs can contain questions, remarks, favorite parts, ideas that you think you will use in other parts of the portfolio, and so on.

♦ Phase Two

Approximately two to four pages, consisting of *typewritten rewrites* of the best parts of your log. This may consist of independent paragraphs, lists, or full essays. Phase two should show that you took the best of your ideas and fashioned them into a more formal presentation.

THEMES, MOTIFS, RECURRENT IMAGES

This section will consist of essays that explain, by giving examples and interpretations, particular items on the list of Shakespearean themes that follows. Select two themes from the list, which you will then carry through the three plays. Organize the section as follows:

♦ Two to four pages on *Julius Caesar,* covering two themes.

♦ Four to six pages on *Julius Caesar* and *Othello* that build on what you wrote for *Julius Caesar* by adding examples of these themes that you find in *Othello.*

♦ Six to eight pages on *Julius Caesar, Othello,* and *The Tempest* that discuss how your themes operate in all three plays.

Shakespearean Themes

mistaken identity	misdelivered messages
uncertainty	dreams and nightmares
tyrrany	stars
intoxication/drugs/states of unreality	storms
witchcraft	retribution and revenge
betrayal	leadership
false accusation	destiny
greed and corruption	abandonment
parents and children	reality vs. illusion
savagery	honor
forgiveness and lack of forgiveness	acting on impulse
superstition	thought vs. action
disease	gardens
self-control and self-understanding	spying
paranoia	

PHRASE COLLECTIONS (INVENTORY)

- Phase One

  Keep a list of phrases that interest you as you read the plays. Your inventory should contain at least 100 items in total.

- Phase Two

  Take these 100 phrases and group them into several categories. You will have to decide which kinds of categories the phrases can fall into. Your list of themes might give you some ideas.

- Phase Three

  Use several of these phrases in a given category to write a description of an aspect of nature or life that is characterized by some sort of uncertainty, irony, or mixed elements. Integrate the phrases in as natural a way as possible, but italicize them. (two pages)

COMPARISONS

Consider the first scene in any of the five acts (or, the last scene in any of the five acts.) Compare what is happening at this point in each of the three plays. Express these similarities in a chart (table).

REFLECTION

Your Shakespeare Portfolio will obviously represent a considerable commitment of time and energy. You will have three *reflection* pieces, one page each, in the portfolio:

- Phase One—Before

  Before we begin (now), reflect on how you think you will handle this project, what you think you will learn, how you will have to manage your time, the level of difficulty that you think it represents, your attitude about doing it, and so on.

- Phase Two—During

  Halfway through *Othello*, reflect on the progress you are making, whether you think you are *on target*, what you've learned so far, how you need to approach the balance of the project, any surprises (positive or negative) that you've encountered.

♦ Phase Three—After

Reflect on the entirety of the project, what you have learned, how you have grown as a learner, how you can use what you've done in future writing or learning projects. Consider not only the Shakespearean content of the project, but also the time management and *habits of mind* skills that you've put into practice. Assess your strengths and weaknesses as a learner.

ADDITIONAL DIRECTIONS

♦ I highly recommend that you purchase copies of the three Shakespearean texts, preferably the Cambridge editions. With your own copy, you can make notations and highlights that will be useful.

♦ Your portfolio will be collected every two weeks (Fridays) so that I can check your progress.

INSTRUCTION

The Shakespeare portfolio is done mostly outside of class. It works out well for the portfolio to be homework because all of the reading of the plays should be done in class. It is not a good idea to ask students to go home and read Shakespeare. The plays have to come alive in class, through the various performance tasks like the ones shown here.

STANDARDS, CHALLENGE LEVEL, MULTIPLE INTELLIGENCES

The Shakespeare portfolio outlined here is a comprehensive project that meets numerous Standards, is highly challenging and calls upon multiple intelligences. In the form that it's in, where students have to do every part, I recommend it only for high-level classes. However, it can certainly be adapted and scaled down to include fewer plays and fewer components. In a heterogeneous class, you might want to establish contracts, differentiating instruction for ability groups. With a contract, students can select among *work plans*, each worth a set amount of points. A student can contract to have more time, fewer tasks, double-up on one task and omit another, or work with two plays rather than three. I find that it takes at least three or four weeks to do justice to a Shakespearean play, working within a traditional high school nonblock schedule.

SUMMARY

English teachers find that teaching Shakespeare is one of the most challenging, and also one of the most rewarding, endeavors. The tasks shown here are designed to make the Shakespearean experience accessible and memorable by engaging the student in performance as well as in personal reflection.

REFERENCES

ATEG (Assembly for the Teaching of English Grammar, and affiliate of the National Council of Teachers of English). (1999, July 16). *Scope, sequence and standards project: Progress report.* Presented at the Annual Meeting in Raritan, NJ.

Glatthorn, A. A. (1999). *Performance standards & authentic learning.* Larchmont, NY: Eye on Education.

Danielson, C., & Marquez, E. (1998). *A collection of performance tasks and rubrics: High school mathematics.* Larchmont, NY: Eye on Education.

Darling-Hammond, L., & Falk, B. (1997, November). Using standards and assessments to support student learning. *Phi Delta Kappan.*

International Reading Association/National Council of Teachers of English Standards Document. http://www.ncte.org/standards/

Lazear, D. (1994). *Multiple intelligence approaches to assessment: solving the assessment conundrum.* Tuscon, AZ: Zephyr Press.

Noddings, N. (1997, November). Thinking about standards. *Phi Delta Kappan,* 184–189.

Popham, W. J. (1997, October). What's wrong and what's right with rubrics. *Educational Leadership,* 72–75.

Seward, T. (Ed.). (1988). *Shakespeare: Julius Caesar.* New York: Cambridge University Press.

Standards Composite reprinted from *Literary Cavalcade,* a Scholastic, Inc. publication. *Literary Cavalcade* is published eight times per year by Scholastic, Inc., 555 Broadway, New York, NY 10012. Used with permission of the publisher.

Vavra, E. (1999, July). Williamsport, PA: Pennsylvania College of Technology. http://webmail.pct.edu/courses/evavra/ENL111/insM/Mic.htm.

Wald, M. L. (1998, June 5). Setting limits on teen-age drivers. *New York Times.*